(?)

Pr

THE BOOKER BOOK

THE BOOKER BOOK

by Simon Brett

SIDGWICK & JACKSON
LONDON

First published in Great Britain in 1989 by Sidgwick & Jackson Limited

ISBN 0-283-99631-5

Typeset by Hewer Text Composition Services, Edinburgh
Printed in Great Britain by Billing & Sons Ltd, Worcester
for Sidgwick & Jackson Limited
1 Tavistock Chambers, Bloomsbury Way
London WC1A 2SG

To my friends in publishing
(while I still have some)

1969

The Booker Prize had a greater effect on Geraldine Byers than anything else in her life.

And it is my privilege to be allowed to chronicle that life. Though I, Mary Mott, am insignificant, untouched by genius myself, it has been my good fortune to rub shoulders with genius. From schooldays onwards I have known – dare I say even been a close friend of – Geraldine Byers, the writer. And she has graciously consented, notwithstanding my unfamiliarity with the skills of biography, that I should be – as she put it, flattering me as ever – Mrs Gaskell to her Charlotte Brontë.

The narrative that follows is therefore written with Geraldine Byers' blessing, and no biographer could have wished for more selfless cooperation from his or her subject. Geraldine has talked to me unstintingly, given me access to papers, diaries, letters, even let me read her Work-in-Progress on many occasions over the last twenty years. If this book gives a less-than-complete picture of Geraldine Byers, the failing must be attributed to my inadequacy as a chronicler rather than to any reticence or evasiveness on her part.

I could give a full and exhaustive history of Geraldine's early years, of life at the girls' boarding school in Gloucestershire where I first had the privilege of meeting her, but I know that the biographer must be selective and will therefore concentrate on those twenty years of her adult life which were of greatest significance in my subject's development as a writer.

In 1968, at the age of twenty-six, Geraldine Byers had had one novel respectably and respectfully published by the small family-owned house of Abrams & Willis. The book, entitled *Pale Cast of Thought*, had not been greeted by huge media attention, but the general tone of its reception had been welcoming. The *Stroud Advertiser*, no less, heralding the arrival of a new local author (her parents lived in Gloucestershire), had hailed the book as 'promising'. I was lucky enough to have been given a proof copy by Geraldine herself and, though I can't claim to have understood all of it, I thought it was frightfully clever.

1

The book had not done anything vulgar, like selling in large quantities, and so, after publication, Geraldine Byers was ideally poised – had she wished to follow that course – to become a literary figure, to write the odd review, to lecture on creative writing, and to join committees – some of whose members didn't live in NW1 – dedicated to the concerns of the literary establishment.

But it was not in Geraldine's nature to be content with such facile celebrity; she knew that the next step forward in her own writing was more important. While she saw many examples of the ease with which one can remain a literary figure without actually writing anything, there was within her a sense of destiny, a gnawing urge to get words down on paper. She wanted to be not just a literary figure, but a major literary figure – a distinguished novelist, in fact.

(This desire, I hasten to point out, was not motivated by anything so crude as mere ambition. Geraldine had realized early on the responsibilities of genius. To let a talent like hers lie unused would be an insult to whatever power it was that had given her that talent.)

One potential impediment to the realization of her literary aims was the fact that, as a writer, she had nothing to say. But few authors in the past, present or – one can safely assume – future have allowed that consideration to inhibit them, and Geraldine was not the woman to be daunted by such a detail. Her own extensive reading and her English course at Cambridge had taught her many of the ways in which absence of content could be disguised by the cosmetic application of style; and her one published book had contrived to confuse readers by reverberating uncannily, but indefinably, with the cadences of other writers.

(To intrude a personal note here, I would like to say that I was one of the first to see Geraldine Byers' creative process at work. I was privileged to have her sitting next to me both for A-Levels at school and for Cambridge Final examinations and, while I slaved away, was aware of her more leisured approach to the task in hand. She always seemed to have time to smile encouragement to me and take an interest in what I was writing. By coincidence we gained identical marks in both examinations – about as close as I ever came to matching her genius!)

The difficulty Geraldine encountered as she approached the north face of her second novel was selecting the style which should be echoed in this latest *oeuvre*. She had amorphous, as yet unspecific, ideas of what the book would be about – she did not like to use the word 'plot', feeling it to be a crude concept more appropriate to category fiction than to the major literary work she had in mind – but she was undecided about the form her new novel should take.

'God, it's hell being a writer,' she said during her endless mastication of this problem, 'absolute hell.' She said this frequently to me; she said it to Mo, her live-in lover; she said it to her colleagues at *Pivot* magazine; she said it to her parents when she went down to visit them in Gloucestershire; she said it, in fact, to anyone who would listen.

And, as she sat, for those magic, dedicated hours between seven and nine every morning, gazing out over the gentrified backstreets of Notting Hill from the window of the flat her parents had bought her, chewing the end of her green Venus 2B pencil and occasionally looking down at the accusingly blank feint-ruled lines of her latest orange-covered school exercise book, she said it quite a lot to herself. 'God, it's hell being a writer,' she would say to herself, alternating the thought with that other *mantra* of her existence: 'It's a terribly lonely life being a writer.'

She was fully aware of the Mephistophelean contract which must be entered into by all creative artists. She knew that one has to suffer for art, and during those endless, agonizingly unproductive mornings, she felt confident that she was paying her dues in suffering. The art, she hoped, would follow.

God, it *was* difficult, though. I have heard Geraldine talking on the subject at great length on many occasions, but I feel I only understand a small part of the difficulty a true writer faces. Geraldine knew the sort of writer she wanted to be, that was easy. She wanted to be the sort of writer who took the world of letters by storm, whose latest work was hailed as 'a breath of fresh air through the dusty corridors of the literary establishment'.

She could go further than that in detailing the kind of praise that would be lavished on her second book. Indeed, one of her favourite pastimes was composing the reviews it would receive. I have found in her early notebooks examples of these literary *jeux d'esprit*. 'Geraldine Byers' new book shows the way forward for the English novel.' 'The authentic voice of the sixties is at last being heard; and it is a voice that will continue to reverberate through the seventies.' 'What an astonishing and refreshing talent we have in Geraldine Byers!' If the notebooks are anything to go by, she spent many hours in rephrasing and polishing such sentences. In fact I found many more examples of these accolades than of the sentences of the *oeuvre* which was to prompt them. But then for a great writer no form of literary experimentation is ever wasted; it is all part of the creative evolutionary process.

So, though Geraldine knew exactly what she wanted it to be, the novel itself remained resolutely unwritten.

'God, it's hell being a writer,' she would murmur to Mo, as they drew apart after the latest unlikely coupling he had read about in *Forum* magazine (they were, needless to say, a very liberated couple), 'trying to get across what you've got to say, in a way that actually *says* it to the reader.'

(I should point out that, though I was obviously not present at these intimate moments – and indeed many other less intimate moments of her life – Geraldine's frankness in evoking such scenes to me and her altruistic willingness that I should recreate them have made their inclusion in my narrative very easy. And the fact that I myself have never experienced comparable intimate delights has made an interesting challenge for my own modest skills as a writer!)

'Yeah,' Mo would say, half-hearing Jimi Hendrix on the hi-fi and watching the smoke from their shared post-coital joint spiral upwards to the navy-blue-emulsioned ceiling, 'yeah. You don't have to tell me, babe.'

Mo did not resent her constant reiteration of what hell it was being a writer, because he knew all about it. He had comparable, though different, problems with his poetry. The composition he found almost embarrassingly easy; it was getting the stuff published that proved impossible. Of course, he didn't care from the financial point of view – he had a proper contempt for money and all its trappings (which is why he didn't like to cheapen his relationship with Geraldine by offering her any rent for the flat) – but he craved the kick of seeing his post-Liverpool *pensées* in print. Because of the unaccountable lack of enthusiasm from established publishers, he was even giving quite serious consideration to the idea of setting up a press to disseminate his work and that of a few like-minded friends. 'Peace and Love Books', he thought might be a good name. But he didn't want to rush into all that hassle of administration and commercialism. Keep it simple, he reckoned, a bit on the lines of the Beatles' Apple set-up.

However, constant assertions of what hell it was being a writer did not make Geraldine's dilemma go away. Sometimes, she confided to me, after Mo had fallen into his sated sleep, she would lie awake under the sheets and blankets of the floor-level mattress they shared for a full ten minutes, agonizing about her writing.

The second book, she knew, had to be the big one, had to be definitive. It had to be the one that put her into her proper niche in the pantheon of young British novelists, but still she couldn't decide in what style it should be written. One can understand the depths of her frustration. The same question kept recurring in her fevered mind: on whom should she model herself this time? If only there existed some standard, some literary yardstick against which her efforts could be measured. She needed a sign from heaven that would tell her definitively what sort of book she should write.

For Geraldine Byers, the Booker Prize was to prove to be that sign from heaven.

She first heard about the prize at work. *Pivot* was a monthly magazine about matters literary, which plumed itself on its esoteric approach and its dwindling circulation. The editor, Robin Troke-Nuttall, had formerly worked in the BBC Radio Features Department, where his days had been punctuated by morning coffee and afternoon tea and almost eclipsed by long lunches with contributors. He brought this management style to the Bloomsbury offices of *Pivot*. He was coherent but foul-tempered for the two hours between ten-thirty and twelve-thirty in the mornings, in the afternoons genial but incoherent for the hour and a half between four (when he returned from lunch) and five-thirty (when the pubs reopened). Geraldine's job was to bring his morning coffee (in bone china with Nice biscuits on a plate) and his afternoon tea (similarly presented), to listen in to his afternoon phone-calls and make a note of the articles he commissioned (because he would never remember them in the morning), and (particularly in the afternoon) to evade his amiable hand up her miniskirt. The rest of her time was devoted to desultory reading of a wide range of newspapers and periodicals, snipping out with a pair of engraved nail-scissors any reports or articles which might be thought to be of interest to the readers of *Pivot*.

The work suited her well. It was not onerous, because a silent girl of unusual ugliness did all the typing and accounts. (Geraldine has always had this wonderful ability to get other people to deal with the mundane details of day-to-day living, so that she is not distracted from the seething creativity of her unique imagination.) And working at *Pivot* gave Geraldine the reassuring feeling of being in an artistic milieu. Though she could not actually write in the office, she had plenty of time there to think and plan. And, since *Pivot* was an oasis for a great many indigent contributors, hungry for its coffee and telephones, and since the magazine was on the list for most publishers' parties, she breathed the oxygen of daily mixing with other writers, so important in the apprenticeship of a major novelist.

Robin Troke-Nuttall spoke of himself as a writer, though the day when he last put words on paper was shrouded in the mists of history. He was, however, solemnly and frequently said to be working on a definitive life of Dylan Thomas. The poet had apparently been sick over his tweeds more frequently than over those of any other producer in the Radio Features Department, so Robin was reckoned to be uniquely qualified for this weighty biographical undertaking. (Thank goodness my qualification for writing Geraldine's life did not involve such unpleasantness!) But, since there was not an evening of the week when he didn't weave his way back to his Fitzrovia flat after closing time, and since he spent his weekends staying with a variety of 'chums in the country', when Robin actually did any writing on his major project remained a mystery.

It was in her daily trawling of the press, in 1968 as a matter of fact, that Geraldine first encountered a reference to the prize which was to change her life. For most readers of the item the striking feature would probably have been the sum of money involved. £5,000 was a great deal in those days, a plutocrat's annual income, certainly way beyond the aspirations of any novelist save those who committed the literary solecism of bestsellerdom. But for Geraldine Byers, money was not important; she devoutly shared Mo's disdain for materialism; besides, she had a private income.

No, what excited her much more about the announcement was the thought that now some objective valuation might enter into the world of letters. No longer would she have to piece together her literary opinions from the vagaries of conflicting critics; soon there would be a prize which gave an authentic *imprimatur* of success to its winner. Even from that first moment, the seed of ambition was sown. Geraldine Byers now knew her literary destiny; she would win the Booker Prize.

Though not overly afflicted by self-doubt, Geraldine had within her a strong core of realism, and she accepted that her ambition might take a little while to achieve. A year or two might be necessary before she could see exactly what kind of book the judges chose, before she had honed her own style to coincide precisely with their specifications, but she felt confident that the achievement was within her grasp.

Caught up in the excitement of the moment, she took the cutting straight through to Robin Troke-Nuttall's office. It was nearly five and he was sleeping off the day's lunch, slumped back in his swivel chair, a plump bundle of tweed, purring with rhythmic snores, for all the world like a large ginger cat.

Years of training at the BBC had paid off, and his eyes opened instantly at the sound of the door. By the time Geraldine had closed it, the telephone receiver was in his hand. 'No,' he was saying, 'no, Julian, I think it's just the *wrong* time for a reassessment of Galsworthy. Everyone would think that we had only thought of it because of this wretched *Forsyte Saga* on the television. Literature must keep itself free from the taint of these new barbarities. No, sorry, Julian – goodbye!'

And then he spoiled it all by missing the cradle as he slammed the receiver down.

However, he was in the genial part of his cycle, so, rather than castigating her for the interruption, all he did was to smile benignly at Geraldine and ask, 'What is it, my dear?'

'I thought you'd be interested to see this.'

She put the cutting down on his blotter, and moved neatly back before his alcohol-retarded hand could land on the curve of her buttock. While he read, she looked at herself in the mirror over Robin's fireplace where the gas-fire burned. She smoothed her hair down from its centre parting and offset the knot of the Indian silk scarf round her neck. Geraldine has far too fine a nature to be afflicted by vanity, but, as she has often said to me, 'Of course it's not something that would ever worry you, but if one is blessed with exceptional good looks, it is difficult to be unaware of the fact.'

'Vulgar,' Robin Troke-Nuttall pronounced.

'What?'

'This idea of novels becoming part of some kind of horse-race.'

'Oh, but surely, Robin, it can do nothing but good. Confer a kind of seal of approval on the English novel. Like the Prix Goncourt.'

'Only a nation as simplistic as the French want seals of approval. English novelists don't need that kind of cheap display.'

'What do they need then?' asked Geraldine cautiously.

'The respect of their fellow-writers.'

'And of their readers . . . ?'

'Well, I suppose that doesn't hurt, but obviously their fellow-writers are more important.'

'Why?'

'Because,' he explained patiently, 'readers are unlikely to review their books, aren't they? Only a novelist's fellow-writers do that.'

But Geraldine's character was too strong to allow Robin Troke-Nuttall's arguments to divert her from her chosen course. The attraction of the Booker Prize as a magnet for her literary ambitions grew and grew. Through the newspapers and periodicals on her desk she traced the preparations for the first award. She noted with interest that the list of thirty-one publishers who had submitted novels did not include Abrams & Willis. This, she concluded, was not necessarily bad news. The lack of other suitable novelists on their list might give a better chance of nomination to her great work when it was completed. But, even if the absence of Abrams & Willis from the roll of nominations implied some internal inefficiency, the thought of changing publishers did not occur to her. In those days a publisher was regarded in the same light as a family solicitor or a bank; one stayed with the house which published one's first effort.

Fortunately, because *Pivot* reviewed books, all of the latest publications appeared in the office, and so Geraldine was able to read the six shortlisted novels before the first award was made. She had to be quick to achieve this; Robin Troke-Nuttall's habit when commissioning reviews was to tell his reviewers to pick up another copy from the publishers and then take all the office booty down to a shop in the Charing Cross Road, where the books were converted into pounds, shillings and pence, which provided a welcome – and necessary – subsidy for his drinking. Just as the editor of *Pivot* had never been seen to write a word of a book, he had never been seen to read one either.

Because of her sense of destiny, Geraldine Byers' level of excitement about the award of the first Booker Prize was probably higher than that of most of the literary establishment. Publishers were then – as now – a traditional breed, and long habit had trained them to suspicion of the new; they were prepared to wait and see how the prize turned out before manifesting any unseemly enthusiasm for it.

But Geraldine was deeply concerned about the fate of what increasingly she came to think of as *her* prize. She weighed up the qualities of the six shortlisted books and, after lengthy deliberation, decided that, had she been consulted, the first Booker Prize should be awarded to Muriel Spark's *The Public Image*.

Under normal circumstances, confident that all the dailies would be on her desk when she arrived in the office, she did not buy a newspaper, preferring to read novels on the tube journey between Notting Hill Gate and Tottenham Court Road, but on the morning of 23 April 1969, flushed with excitement, she went straight from the flat to her local newsagent, a sixpence and a threepenny bit at the ready in her hand. She bought *The Times* and found on Page Two the news she sought.

At the Draper's Hall the previous night Dame Rebecca West had handed over a trophy and cheque for £5,000 to the first winner of the Booker Prize, P. H. Newby, for his novel, *Something to Answer For*.

Undeterred by the failure of her selection, that lunch-hour Geraldine Byers went to the London Library and took out all of the books she could find on modern Egypt.

The weekend following the award she spent at her parents' Cotswold-stone house in Gloucestershire. Notting Hill flat life was of course great fun, and she thoroughly approved of Mo's resistance to material values, but she very sensibly recognized the creative artist's need for a little pampering from time to time.

And her parents, as I frequently witnessed through my schooldays, were very good at pampering their only daughter. Though Geraldine disapproved of wealth as a general principle, she was too soft-hearted and loyal to condemn her Aged Parents for theirs. It was not the poor A.P.s' fault, after all, she reasoned. Mr Byers had worked jolly hard being a stockbroker and he couldn't help the fact that he'd been jolly good at it. It would have been plain perverse for him not to have used his accumulated expertise with his own money, and one couldn't withhold a sneaking admiration for the success of his chosen investments. It wasn't as if her parents spent irresponsibly, after all. Her mother made a lot of jam and things for distribution to distressed local pensioners, so the wealth was being recycled into the community.

I understood Geraldine's arguments completely, but Mo found them less persuasive, and so now, by mutual agreement, he stayed in London when she went down to the country. This was probably no bad thing. His presence, with hair down to his shoulders, in flared jeans, buttoned T-shirt and granny glasses had always struck an incongruous note in Gloucestershire. And, as Geraldine confided to me with typical frankness, she could never suppress a slight feeling of relief at a weekend's separation from him. Mo made her constantly aware of the gulf between the ideals she shared with him and the life-style her parents enjoyed; when he was not there, she had no difficulty in slipping back into her childhood role in the family home.

And, yes, that role did involve a degree of pampering. But always, as she lay waiting for sleep in her snug little bedroom, sinking into the mattress on a properly-sprung divan, looking across at her own little curtained dressing table, up to the silhouette frieze of Cinderella, Baron Hardup, the Ugly Sisters, Buttons and Prince Charming that her father had had made for her fifth birthday, and down to the phalanx of cuddly toys on the floor, she felt very secure and right.

It was good to know that she would be woken on Saturday morning by her mother bringing her breakfast in bed; good to know that she would go riding in the afternoon; good, even, that her parents would have arranged a dinner party for the evening. She recognized of course that that would be a frightful occasion in many ways for someone as liberated as Geraldine Byers, but she reckoned she could cope. Even though the people would all be dreadfully square. Often her parents and their friends even dressed for dinner!

She knew that I was likely to be invited. And no doubt George, whose parents also lived locally, would be present. George, in an era of her life Geraldine had expunged totally from her memory (but which I remembered rather well), had accompanied her to Young Conservative 'hops'. George, whom Mo had dubbed 'Mr Suit' one rather awkward weekend when the two of them had met in Gloucestershire.

Poor old George, thought Geraldine, charitable as ever, it wasn't really fair. He couldn't help the fact that he was in chemicals or that he was deeply boring or that he never read a book. (I have to admit at this point that these qualities of George's never worried me. To me he just seemed a friendly and rather good-looking man. But then, as I have come increasingly to recognize, mine is an infinitely less sensitive nature than Geraldine's.)

Anyway – to resume the painstaking recreation of my subject's interior monologue – Geraldine comforted herself with the thought that Mo wouldn't be there the following evening, so she could forget what a grotty occasion it really was and just enjoy the dinner party. Her mother had a wonderful cook and her father's cellar was quite exceptional.

As she drifted into childlike sleep, with one last look up to the outlines of her Cinderella frieze, Geraldine Byers felt wonderfully secure. It wasn't just the prospect of a weekend of pampering that gave her that feeling. She had also reached a major watershed in her creative life. She now knew the style in which her second novel would be written.

All that remained for her to do was to write it.

It was not easy. Writing's never easy, Geraldine kept telling herself, as she read and planned and tried out and tinkered with a first few tentative sentences of the new novel.

She rang Abrams & Willis and told her editor, Sidney Parrot, that she was under way on a new book. He claimed to be delighted at the news and offered her diffident encouragement. She did not tell him that it was the book that would win the Booker Prize. Better to let him reach that conclusion for himself when he read it.

After a whole week of intensive reading about Egypt, Geraldine felt ready to brazen out the challenge of that empty feint-ruled page. She picked up a green Venus 2B pencil and wrote the momentous words, 'Chapter One'. From now on, she knew, she was not her own woman. She had made the commitment. From that moment onwards, she would be a thing possessed, a mere creature of her own peremptory imagination. The book had got its hooks into her, and over the ensuing months the barbs would dig in deeper and deeper.

After three weeks of frantic early morning activity, Geraldine Byers had made a start on the Booker Book. On the evening of the third Friday she arrived at my flat, exhausted and overwrought. After I had plied her with restorative gin and tonics and cooked dinner for her, she confided in me that that morning she had dared to read back what she had written so far. To my enormous joy and disbelief – for it was more than I had ever dared hope – she asked me if I would like to read the opening chapter.

*

Nothing to Shout About
by G. H. Byers
CHAPTER ONE
THE LAST REFUGE

The old girl kept on at him and he knew he could have done worse. The idea even started Barron on a succession of dreams. In his sleep he drifted through the heat-rippled, maritime city. He could smell the petrol, the dust, the brick, the arrack, the jasmine and the goat. He dreamed that Mrs Iqbal, Ahmed, their two daughters and he sat on canvas chairs on the beach at Port Said while the rippling level of the sand slowly rose around them. He dreamed they were in a dimly-lit bar, surrounded by barrels, heavy with the aniseed reek of ouzo and Cyprus brandy. When the shutters opened, gold dazzled and he had to half-shut his eyes to look across to the buildings that rippled on the other side of the Canal.

Mrs Iqbal kept writing to say that they were both alone now and that friends were hard to come by and that if he were to fly out to her on a jet he would see for himself how suitable the arrangement could be; because the Revolution and the departure of the troops from the Canal Zone did not mean that the Egyptians no longer respected the English. They were both unattached. In spite of her marriage to the deceased Ahmed, she was still of the same nationality as Barron. Her proposition made good sense.

The suggestion amused him. True, he was alone. His wife was no longer alive and in some ways that was a relief. Their daughter Cindy was almost old enough to cease to be a financial liability, but that didn't mean things were easy. Times were hard.

Ahmed had probably left his affairs in a mess, but Mrs I. must still be quite flush. It would be a pity if the two hideous daughters were allowed to squander all of the money their father had picked up one way and another. The old girl did need someone to advise her. In fact, she needed someone to manage her affairs now she was on her own. He could not deny that he was tempted.

Until he slipped on the stairs and fell against the front door of the Iqbal flat in 1946 Barron had not felt strongly about the issues of home rule for Egypt or anti-Semitism. But for one moment as the door fell open, balanced on his left cheek and elbow, he saw, upside down, the three women and Ahmed. Through the window the sky rippled with evening after-glow. Ahmed's surprised eyes rose from the gold and ivory toothpick with which he was cleaning his fingernails.

For one moment Barron thought the daughters must be the two most beautiful women alive. As they rose, alarmed by his entrance, he saw their thick, rippling calves and pouting breasts against the red

11

clouds. Beyond the black silhouette of the balcony railing the outlines of hotels diluted and were lost in the rippling sky that climbed steeply above Port Said. White-sailed feluccas skimmed across the water which the sunset washed with pinks and golds. Brick, dust, wood, hay, dung, ouzo, leather, drains, jasmine and goat breathed sensuality into him. He heard all Egypt, from the subtle splash of a crocodile into the Nile to the erratic tick of the meter of a Cairo taxi. These were no ordinary girls.

Either his eyes readjusted to the light or the beauty of the daughters was a vision because Barron now saw them for what they were. Like their mother, they were of a solid, striking ugliness. Ahmed spoiled them. He gave them silk dresses, ropes of pearls, alligator-hide handbags, bottles of perfume, combs set in diamonds, boxes of dates, dried figs, anchovies on toast and Turkish Delight stuffed with nuts and cream. Their figures bore testimony to his generosity.

As he brushed his teeth Barron looked out over the grey wet roof tops of Hampstead. It was a cold day. So far as the bloody office was concerned he was on holiday. He was on two weeks' holiday. Well, he *was*, wasn't he? Yes, he was. He bloody well was. It wouldn't matter if that stretched to three weeks, a month. Cindy was old enough to look after herself for that long.

Mrs I., in spite of being an ugly, tough old trot, was a rich widow. Why should he feel guilty for what his government had or hadn't done about Hitler? Or about Nasser, come to that? Or Ahmed Iqbal? Or Cleopatra? Or Tutankhamun? Or any of the other confused and suffering people of the Canal Zone? What was wrong with remarrying? Perhaps it would be no bad thing.

1970

Throughout the rest of 1969 Geraldine worked on the book, but her progress was slow. Writing, rewriting, three steps forward, two steps back. The orange-covered feint-ruled school exercise books filled and were then scored over with crossings-out and emendations. She confided in me that sometimes, in moments of despair, she even questioned the wisdom of modelling her style on that of P. H. Newby, even contemplated throwing away everything she had done and starting out on a completely new novel. Thank goodness, she was strong enough to resist such blasphemous thoughts. She knew that writing a book was like Christ's forty days and nights in the wilderness; that the Devil would offer her many forms of temptation to give up the whole project; and that the test of her stature as a writer was her ability to keep going even when every argument of logic and mental exhaustion screamed against such a course. No, through all the long, long vigil of the actual writing she kept her eyes fixed on the Holy Grail of the Booker Prize.

The writing was still restricted to those sacred two hours every morning. The rest of her life followed its predictable course. She continued her work at *Pivot*. Robin Troke-Nuttall did little to disguise his disappointment when the miniskirt gave way to the maxi; he tried for a while to transfer his attentions from Geraldine's bottom to her breasts, but his heart wasn't in it; hard to teach an old dog new tricks, and he was a lifetime bottom-man. He became more lugubrious; even his afternoon bonhomie was muted, and in the mornings there was no speaking to him. For the first time the accelerating diminution of *Pivot*'s circulation seemed to worry him. Inflation apparently took its toll on the second-hand value of review copies, and on more than one occasion he claimed to have run out of small change and wondered if Geraldine could lend him a pound note. Or a fiver would be even better . . .

Pivot remained on the list for publishers' parties, and Geraldine stayed close to the epicentre of the literary world. I would hear about her glittering social round on those occasional evenings when she appeared on my doorstep for a meal, an unexpected but ever-welcome guest. She went to one party which was also attended by Iris Murdoch and Kingsley Amis, though she didn't actually speak to either of them. She was invited to another where Gore Vidal was said to have been a guest, though that might just have been a rumour.

Her weekends were also full. If in London, she spent the time with friends denouncing materialism; if in the country, enjoying its benefits. On London Saturdays she would go to the Kensington High Street Biba (not yet transferred to the magnificent folly of the Derry & Toms building), to browse, occasionally to buy, most of all just to be there. She might subsequently move on to Way In at Harrods; it depended on her mood. I was occasionally included in these jaunts and, as she tried on garment after garment, could only marvel once again at how much better clothes hung on her tall, willowy frame than on my short, dumpy one. Mo occasionally criticized her for trying to dress younger than she was, but she put his murmurings about 'mutton-dressed-as-lamb' down to simple jealousy. She had noticed the half-crown-size tonsure beginning at the centre of his long locks, and some of his chest hairs were white.

She talked to me a lot over that period about her relationship with Mo, which was not running as smoothly as it had done. Apparently he kept saying that property was theft and that they ought to move into a squat. He showed no signs of actually leaving the flat her father had bought though his raising of the subject was perhaps indicative of a potential rift between them. He also started to see – well, no, more than see – to have affairs with other women.

He was very open about this. He and Geraldine discussed it – or perhaps if 'discuss' is a word with too much connotation of mutuality about it, I should say that he told her all about it. He told her that sex was a very beautiful thing, that bodies were for sharing, that exclusive physical relationships were just another form of imperialism, and that jealousy was very bad *karma*. While accepting the validity of all these arguments, Geraldine did not feel absolutely convinced by them, and could not totally suppress a very uncool reaction to his behaviour, namely one of anger.

She came to the conclusion that two could play at that game, and one weekend in Gloucestershire decided to give George the treat of his life by going to bed with him. Pill-protected, she felt sublimely confident that she could shudder the foundations of his 'squareness' and teach him a thing or two. In the event, George sprung the surprise by teaching her a thing or two. Geraldine stored the knowledge of the episode as a potential weapon to attack Mo when the need arose. Imperialism it may have been, but she was determined at least not to be an unarmed imperialist.

(I have to confess that, when she first told me of this incident, my reaction was also rather uncool because I had been under the

14

impression that I was George's girlfriend at the time. We hadn't gone to bed together, because I believed in saving sex for marriage, but I thought we had some sort of commitment. However, with her customary charm, Geraldine soon persuaded me to see the incident from her point of view. I had to understand how important it was for writers to gain as many varied experiences as possible. And she gently clinched the argument by reminding me that artists cannot be bound by the shackles of conventional morality. Of course, she was right, and she made me feel slightly sheepish for ever having raised the subject.)

Mo's plans to start his own publishing business were at last developing. He kept holding late grass-scented meetings in Geraldine's flat, when, while Janis Joplin shrieked from the hi-fi, earnest discussions took place about the likelihood of printers giving their services free, and the desirability of books having no prices on them so that purchasers could give whatever they thought appropriate. 'I mean,' I once heard Mo say, 'like, if someone wants just to give a flower, well, that's great. I mean, if the flower means something to them, you know, if they're saying: "This flower is a beautiful thing, that book is a beautiful thing, let's exchange these beautiful things", well, that's where it's at, isn't it?'

The T-shirted assembly of experimental poets, novelists and former psychedelic illustrators nodded their shaggy heads, stressed the importance of love in literature, and started to draw up lists of which capitalist publishers would be first to the wall come the Revolution.

But Mo was eventually faced by one of the incontrovertible facts of the book trade: that you cannot start a publishing house on love alone.

'Gerry,' he said one evening when the three of us got back to the flat after seeing *Easy Rider*, 'you know you got quite a lot of bread . . .'

She was in the kitchen, showing me where the spaghetti was for supper, and didn't hear him. 'What?'

'Gerry, I was saying, like, you've got a lot of bread, you know, from your parents . . .'

She was forced to concede that she had. 'I mean, not that much, really, Mo, but a bit, I suppose, yes.'

'Well, a lot compared to what a starving kid in Biafra's got.'

'All right, I accept that.'

'Look, like, I've seen a way you could, like, sort of salve your conscience about it.'

'About the money?'

'Yes.'

'But I haven't got a conscience about it.'

'Oh, come *on*.'

She quickly corrected herself. 'That is to say, obviously I have a bit, but — '

'Well, listen, babe, suppose you put some of the bread into setting me up . . . ?'

'Setting you up?'

'Yeah, in this publishing business. We got some great ideas for the first lot of books. I mean, apart from my poems. There's this Squatter's Cookbook . . . you know, like how to make meals when the power's switched off . . . And Chad's going to do this series of *haikus* about the Mylai massacre . . . Then there's this astrological calendar for motorcycles and a Red Brigade bomb-making manual and — '

'Yes, all right, Mo, they're great ideas, but I don't really see where I fit in.'

'You put up the money.'

'Oh.'

'Get us started.'

'I see.'

'And then, you know, when we got enough bread, we pay you back.'

'With profits?' she asked instinctively.

Mo looked pitying. 'I don't know, Gerry. Those parents of yours really *scarred* you with their capitalist ideas, didn't they?'

She was stung. I always thought she looked rather magnificent when she was angry. 'It was those capitalist ideas which bought this flat where you live rent-free!'

He shook his head. The hair brushed his shoulders despairingly. 'Gerry, Gerry . . . Why is it that you always have to reduce every argument to such trivial details?' He turned to me. 'I don't suppose you've got any bread you fancy putting into a business, have you, Mary?'

I had to confess that I hadn't.

'Don't know anyone else who's loaded, do you?'

'No. Sorry. Well, except George, of course . . .'

Mo snorted his contempt for 'Mr Suit'.

Geraldine told me she'd made him sleep on the sofa that night. Even though he'd apparently learnt this wonderful new foreplay technique from a waitress he'd met at a Jethro Tull gig. And she maintained her refusal to give him a single penny for his publishing venture. She told me it was because she thought he would probably just spend the money on pot, but I believe her reasons were more complex. Geraldine was beginning to wonder whether her relationship with Mo was going to go the distance. And when the break came – if it did – she didn't want the ties between them to be any more complex than they already were.

He appeared to have got the money from somewhere, though, because the pattern of his meetings changed. When I was in the flat one evening a few months later, I noticed that the shaggy heads were nodding over more practical details than before. The hi-fi was switched off. Mo had even forbidden the lighting-up of joints.

And a few weeks later, granted the use of a room over a delicatessen in Notting Hill, he got into the habit of going there every morning, for all the world like a person with a job. Beside the bell-push adjacent to the delicatessen appeared a flowered legend: 'Peace and Love Books'. Geraldine told me, with a hint of bitterness in her voice, that Mo no longer confided all his ideas in her. Though they still lived together and apparently tried gamely – even with a slight degree of desperation – to introduce yet more variations into their sex-life, they were drifting apart.

Geraldine, while not denying this fact, did not let it get to her. She was, she kept reminding herself, a creative artist, and she knew that artists had to put personal relationships behind them in their pursuit of perfection. So, if Mo got 'used' a little in the development of her writing, that was just one of the sacrifices which the commonplace world must offer at the altar of genius.

After all, she was going to win the Booker Prize. She was Geraldine Byers, the writer.

Unfortunately, she was also Geraldine Byers, the rather slow writer. Given only two hours a day of creative endeavour, her progress on *Nothing to Shout About* was not as fast as she had hoped. Clearly, something would have to give. At some point *Pivot* would have to soldier on without her services. Robin Troke-Nuttall would, as she put it to me in one of her inimitable *bon mots*, have to search for buttocks new. But not yet. The *moment critique* had not yet arrived.

The tragic consequence of her perfectionist approach to writing was that she was only just half-way through her novel when she started reading items about the 1970 Booker Prize, and little further advanced when the winner's name was announced.

She set off for a weekend of pampering in Gloucestershire, and reread Bernice Rubens' *The Elected Member*. On the Sunday evening she returned to London and, while I whipped up an omelette for her in my flat, announced what her next step in pursuit of the Booker Prize was going to be.

She would rewrite all she had done of *Nothing to Shout About*. She would change the names, the venue, the whole concept of the novel.

She went to the London Library at lunchtime the following day and took out every book she could find on Jewish immigration into England.

Geraldine has a face of such sensitivity that those who know her well can read in it every nuance of her feelings. And I could see that, with her decision made, she felt a new peace after the creative turmoil of the recent months, a new assurance. This time she knew she was on the right track.

THE UNWANTED GUEST
by
Geraldine Byers
2

Rachel Schmeck was too terrified to open her eyes. She lay still in the hollow of the old mattress, daring only to flex her toes against the bedclothes. Once it had been her parents' bed, a flat divan, with an upholstered headboard, double only in name. Adjacent but separate, they had slept through their thirty-year marriage. When her father had died, three years previously, he had, from that very bed, offered it to her. Her mother had readily moved into Rachel's bedroom, which she now shared with the Rabbi, while Rachel remained imprisoned by the past. She let her hand creep up to feel the dry wrinkles of her face. She touched them sadly, for they confirmed the undeniable fact of her ugliness. The fissures and crevices of her face, were, each one, a mark for each of her forty-six years.

She clenched her eyelids fast together. She knew her fitful sleep was over, but did not want to face that fact. God knows how many more of them would have arrived while she was sleeping. God knows how many would be crawling round on the floor. No, she dared not look. She knew they were there, and the less her family believed in their presence, the more convinced she became. She could see the lizards, and though she kept spraying them with Flit, she was afraid of destroying them, or afraid they might turn into something else. She needed them, because they proved she was sane. Ugly, but sane.

Rabbi Hardupski knew he had to go into Rachel's room to wake her, but he put off the moment. He could not face more hallucinations about lizards. He did not like the smell of Flit either. He sat in the kitchen with his cup of lemon tea, seeing the familiar but faded willow pattern in the cup. He watched as his daughter Corey rubbed the copper ladle from above the kitchen sink to its customary high polish. He noticed her fluffy bunny-rabbit bedroom slippers. She was in her thirties, his Corey, and still wearing fluffy bunny-rabbit bedroom slippers. That, too, hurt him. But he had no time to think of that pain.

'Why I should,' he said bewildered, 'a stepdaughter have who lizards on her bedroom floor sees? Better I a stepdaughter have who a *ganuf*

18

is than who these breakdowns has.' Rabbi Hardupski hung his head. 'Better I a stepdaughter have who does not her head shave when she married gets than one who with psychiatrists all the time is.'

'It will be better when Rachel takes the pills the doctor prescribed, Poppa,' said Corey, businesslike.

'What should I know from pills,' Rabbi Hardupski said wearily.

Corey polished the ladle more vigorously. She found it hard to be sympathetic to Rachel. She hated her stepsister for what Rachel was doing to her father. To her, too, come to that. Rachel was the invalid. Rachel had the breakdowns, while Corey kept the house and ran the shop, with only the boy Buttonstein to help her. The fluffy bunny-rabbit bedroom slippers were Rachel's fault, too. Of course, Corey could have worn something different on her feet. But she would not be the same person if she did not wear the fluffy bunny-rabbit bedroom slippers. She could not break the habit. She resented the guilt that Rachel caused in her. They had nothing in common. Both had had miserable childhoods, but in different families. There was no real obligation. Rabbi Hardupski should not have remarried or, if he had, he should have chosen a new wife who would not die within a year and leave him with two ugly middle-aged stepdaughters. She found herself wishing Rachel dead.

Rabbi Hardupski picked up Rachel's cup from the table. 'I go and wake her will,' he said. 'Then I the doctor call. He more hospitals and drugs prescribes. More hospitals and drugs I need already? And only you and I visit will. Rachel's sister Miriam will not visit. Since she with the *goyim* runs off – not even married to the man is she already – her we do not see. And if I and you to hospitals all days visiting going are, Corey, who will mind the shop?'

'We'll manage, Poppa,' Corey said, trying to make it easier for him. 'We managed the other times. Buttonstein will help.'

Rabbi Hardupski sighed. He shook his head wearily. 'Better than I a stepdaughter who lizards sees have, should I a stepdaughter who her words in the right order puts already have.'

He took the cup of lemon tea upstairs to his stepdaughter's bedroom. Corey looked down at her fluffy bunny-rabbit bedroom slippers.

1971

Writing like Bernice Rubens was uphill work. As Geraldine Byers was to find many times over the next twenty years, it is much easier to adopt the style of a flamboyant writer than one who achieves his or her effects by understatement and precise use of language. I watched, helpless, as the months passed and her precarious new-found calm gave way to mounting desperation. Those two morning hours in the flat became the biggest challenge of her day, her desk a scene of continuous carnage as the feint-lined pages were scored, overscored and torn out, the green Venus 2B pencils chewed to matchwood, and the Roget so continuously consulted that its spine broke. God, I could see then what hell it was being a writer.

Geraldine began seriously to doubt whether *The Unwanted Guest* would ever be completed and, as the year between the Booker Prizes trickled away, she started secretly to long for the new award, for a break to the creative vicious circle in which she had become trapped, for an excuse to stop trying to write her novel. But this hope was soon dashed. Checking through the papers in the *Pivot* office one morning in the December of 1970, she came across the news that the whole administration of the Booker Prize was to be changed. The award was no longer to be made in the spring; from 1971 onwards, it would be an autumn prize. Instead of another four months of agony, Geraldine was faced by nearly ten months of creative frustration. She nearly wept.

It was a difficult year for other reasons, too, reasons with which I, as her exact contemporary, could sympathize. Now undeniably almost thirty, Geraldine Byers was at a stage to assess how she should spend the rest of her life. Not her creative life – the future of that was fortunately preordained – no, the question that worried her was how she should spend the rest of her life *as a woman*.

Such speculation was much in the air. 1970 had seen the publication of Germaine Greer's *The Female Eunuch*, which Geraldine had consumed avidly before passing it on to me. (I have to confess I found some of it a bit strong!) Equal pay had become a political issue; so had the whole issue of Women's Rights. A new seriousness had been brought to the subject; men who made jokes about bra-burning at dinner parties were likely to be shrivelled into embarrassed silence. In America positive action was being taken, and, in its customary dilatory way, England was following the transatlantic example. It was a time when no woman could fail to ask herself where she stood *as a woman*.

That question inevitably raised the corollary of who did she stand *with* as a woman, and, as more and more of her contemporaries got married (even I had got engaged!), Geraldine was made to face even more forcibly the inadequacies of her relationship with Mo.

Peace and Love Books had done surprisingly well in their first year. Though the silence which greeted the proprietor's own poems had been uninterrupted by a single sale, the company had gained some welcome publicity by the banning of its Red Brigade bomb-making manual. But the surprise success had been the astrological calendar of the motorcycle. This month-by-month maintenance guide, full of homely tips on the lines of 'When Venus is passing through the house of Saturn, it might be a good idea to check your wheel-nuts', had proved a runaway seller, bought in large numbers by bike enthusiasts, lovers of the occult, and condescending intellectuals who gave it to their friends as a joke present. The sales were sufficient to enable Mo to announce a much more ambitious list for his second year (a list, incidentally, which contained none of his own work; the subject of Mo's poetry dropped out of his conversation a month after the publication of his collection, and never returned).

But success did not necessarily help his relationship with Geraldine. It meant that he spent more and more time at the Peace and Love Books office (now upgraded from the delicatessen site to the ground floor of a warehouse in Ladbroke Grove), and had more opportunities to meet other women. He started employing increasing numbers of increasingly young and increasingly pretty 'editorial assistants', and on the occasions when she did visit him at work, Geraldine was made to feel distinctly middle-aged and obscurely unwelcome. As 1971 progressed, more and more of Mo's assistants started working in hot-pants and, forewarned by the striking effect her appearance wearing them at *Pivot* had had on Robin Troke-Nuttall, Geraldine grew increasingly suspicious of the activities of Mo's wandering hands. While theirs of course remained an adult relationship, and while she still accepted the infantile nature of sexual jealousy, she now had to consider what Mo's indiscretions did to her self-image *as a woman*.

Clearly, they didn't help it one bit.

There were not only problems in Geraldine's private life: things were not going too well at *Pivot* either. The circulation was spiralling down to an embarrassing level. Bills were not getting paid; the phones were hot with the complaints of aggrieved contributors, landlord's agents, gas and electricity board officials. Robin Troke-Nuttall, whose interludes of coherence were growing shorter and shorter, seemed to lack either the capacity or the will to do anything about the situation. Indeed he exacerbated it by refusing to accept the arrival of the new decimal coinage and continuing to fix his contributors' conjectural fees in guineas.

To add insult to injury, the silent girl who did all the actual work at *Pivot* suddenly announced that she was sick of not being paid on time and stumped out of the office in a righteous clatter of platform heels. The idea of recruiting further staff – and indeed the wherewithal to pay any he did recruit – were beyond Robin Troke-Nuttall, so Geraldine found herself in the demeaning position of actually typing. One can only guess at the depth of the anguish this experience – comparable to Dickens' time in the blacking factory – must have caused to a sensitive soul like hers; it was not for typing that she had directed her considerable intellectual skills into the world of literature.

Though after a time, as its editor became increasingly comatose, she found that she was virtually running *Pivot* single-handed and that achievement gave her a degree of satisfaction, Geraldine Byers could not lose sight of the fact that she did not have the status which should accompany her responsibility. What was worse, any literary figure who came into the *Pivot* office and saw her sitting behind a typewriter would take her for a mere secretary. William Golding came in one day for a meeting with Robin Troke-Nuttall and clearly made that assumption. She could have died of shame.

No, the moment was rapidly and inevitably approaching when Geraldine Byers would have to launch herself on the unsuspecting world as a full-time writer.

Most of the spare mental capacity which was not employed in bending her story to the style of Bernice Rubens was now occupied in devising the best way to make the final break with Mo. Geraldine took me through the available options. Should she follow the humane, adult course – cook him a farewell dinner and spell out the arguments that made their separation inevitable? Or should she give in to passion, vent the accumulated spleen of years by throwing his possessions out into the street and having all the locks changed? She devoted a great deal of time to such pleasurable conjecture.

She was therefore, as she reported to me afterwards, more than a little distressed one summer afternoon when her watching of the Ladies Single Final between Evonne Goolagong and Margaret Court was interrupted by the announcement from Mo that he was moving out.

'Like, I've put some bread into an old house up Ladbroke Grove. Needs a lot of work – had some scruffy herberts squatting in there for the last year – but that meant I got a good price, and the way property's going at the moment I can't miss out in the long term, can I?'

Geraldine mouthed hopelessly as the Centre Court rose to acclaim Miss Goolagong's victory. This was not how she had planned the scene which was now taking place.

'And, you know,' Mo went on, aggravatingly retaining the initiative, 'like we've had some good times, but better to quit while we're ahead, eh? Don't want to crowd each other, do we, babe? You know, sure we'll still meet up, be friends, like, probably still have the occasional nostalgic screw for old times' sake, but it'll be less hassle all round if we split now, don't you reckon? We both need space, don't we? And . . .' he added, without malice, but more infuriatingly than if his words had been malicious, 'I'm sure on your own you're going to have much more chance of finding out where you're at, you know, *as a woman.*'

In the autumn of 1971 Geraldine Byers convinced herself of the irrelevance of men. Women were a self-sufficient sex; they had no need to bow to the yoke of masculine imperialism. She read books about women's strength. She explored the possibilities of masturbation more seriously than she had before; she found them mildly rewarding, but limited. She contemplated the purchase of a vibrator, but was restrained – as I would have been had I ever considered the idea – by the fastidiousness of a girls' boarding school education.

The same early training and recollection of dormitory insults inhibited her experimentation with lesbianism. It was, she recognised with appropriate broadmindedness, a perfectly legitimate alternative, and one that she should try. Women, she knew, understood women's needs better than any crass male bull blundering in the china-shop of the female anatomy, but the fact remained that she had yet to meet a woman she fancied. And the thought of doing that kind of thing to another woman . . . well, at the back of her mind lurked the secret fear that she might spoil the magnificent mutuality of the experience by giggling. (I was actually quite relieved that she came to this conclusion, because I felt just the same about such things and hated the idea of there being any embarrassment or misunderstanding between us!)

It was not a happy autumn for Geraldine, and perhaps I have to take part of the blame for that state of affairs. Selfishly excited by thoughts of my own impending marriage (and, I may as well confess, the impending loss of my virginity!), I probably did not accord my friend the undivided attention that was her right.

So I was unaware how often Geraldine's platform boots clomped mournfully along the streets of London, echoing her inner sadness. I was unaware that she felt herself to be a woman alone, her face blurred by the invisible veil of her martyrdom. At times, though I did not know it till afterwards, her precious sense of rightness, of belonging, was challenged; even her self-esteem, usually impervious to any attack, felt a little dented. A tiny mauve cloud of depression hovered around her all that autumn. She read R. D. Laing's *The Divided Self*, trying very hard to identify, but unfortunately failing.

At times, she told me, it was only the knowledge of her destiny as winner of the Booker Prize that kept her going.

Of that year's shortlist she had favoured either the Doris Lessing or the Elizabeth Taylor, and V. S. Naipaul's win took her by surprise. She had read the book before the announcement of the winner and, as was becoming her custom, took it with her down to Gloucestershire for a recuperative weekend with her parents.

The pampering was up to its usual standard. She rode on the Saturday afternoon, and in the evening her parents once again entertained a group of what Mo would have described as 'capitalist fascists'. I was there. So was George, but Geraldine hardly noticed him. The memory of their sexual encounter was vague, and of course there was no room for men in the life of the new, ascetic, feminist Geraldine Byers.

Her father detected the malaise in his beloved daughter. From birth he had seen to it that she always felt a sense of confidence, the unshakeable knowledge that she was the right person in the right place, and it pained him to see the drifting wraith she had become.

'What is it, old seed-cake? What's the problem?' he asked as they drove in the Rolls to see a new hunter he was contemplating buying. (He reported this conversation to George and me on the Sunday afternoon when Geraldine had gone upstairs for a little lie-down.)

'Oh, just everything, Daddy.'

'Everything?'

'Well . . .' She didn't really want to go into her emotional problems. Nor the issues raised by her new-found feminism. Her father was a dear old thing, but a bit old-fashioned when it came to sexual politics. Safer to keep off the subject. 'No, it's . . . well, I suppose it's work.'

'This *Pivot* business? Look, if anyone's making your life difficult there, I'll see to it that they — '

'No, it's not that, Daddy. It's my writing.'

24

'Ah.' A note of respect came into Mr Byers' voice. His own literary excursions had never gone much further than Denis Wheatley, but he felt a proper awe in the face of his adored daughter's genius.

'I just feel I've got to make a greater commitment to my writing, Daddy.'

'Give up *Pivot*, you mean?'

'That may be necessary.'

'Well, if you do need to, my old Mars Bar, don't hesitate. No difficulty about bumping up the old allowance, you know.'

'That's very sweet of you, but money's not really the problem.' Her words were at least partly true; she was, nonetheless, relieved to have got the money position sorted out before she continued with her main anxiety. 'I just feel I need to be more committed as a writer, need to do more research, put more of myself into what I write.'

'Jolly good show, old kipper. What are you on at the moment, what *magnum opus* is it this time . . . if you don't mind me asking?'

'It's difficult.' It was. V. S. Naipaul's *In A Free State* was made up of a number of stories, all about ethnic dislocation; their settings ranged from India to New York, from the Caribbean to London and Africa. She explained the dilemma to her father, concluding uncertainly, 'I suppose I am fairly well-placed in Notting Hill to research the Caribbean-in-London side of things . . .'

'Good heavens, no,' said her father. 'You don't want to mix with that kind of Johnnie.' Before Geraldine could come in with appropriate liberal remonstration, he continued, 'Tell you what, though – Rollo Pumphrey!'

'Rollo Pumphrey?'

'You remember him. Used to be a partner in the firm. Retired to Jamaica.'

'Oh yes.'

'You fly out there for a holiday. Chance to do a bit of research – and bring some colour back to your pretty little cheeks.'

'But, Daddy — '

'Won't hear a word against the idea, my old bus ticket. It's on, and I'll pay for everything,' Mr Byers enthused, glad to be able to demonstrate his greatest parental skill, that of lavishing money on his daughter.

'Oh, very well, Daddy. If you insist.'

She found Jamaica wonderful after the chill and gloom of London. Rollo Pumphrey proved a lavish host. Geraldine, feeling a little as if she were convalescent after some hitherto unacknowledged breakdown, did not do a great deal. She read and lounged on the verandah of Rollo's mansion, looking out over the deep turquoise of the Caribbean. Black servants kept her continuously supplied with exotic foods and drinks.

The only diversion occurred when George, who had been in Florida on some dreary chemical business, broke his journey home for a couple of days in Jamaica. Out of England, Geraldine's feminist principles did not seem so important, and she let him into her bed. That sort of thing doesn't count when you're abroad, she reassured herself and, besides, boring though he undoubtedly was in every other area of his life, George was rather good at sex. It would be unthinkable for her to sleep with anyone so lacking intellectual credentials in London, but in Jamaica . . . well, no one would ever know.

(She told me all this with her customary candour when she got back, and I have to confess that I was furious. You see, although we still hadn't gone to bed together, George was at that time my fiancé, and in fact the argument which arose when I challenged him with what had happened led to the breaking-off of our engagement. To my shame, I blamed Geraldine for this, and it was some months before I began to see her side of the argument and attempt a reconciliation. She, as warm-hearted as ever, accepted my apologies without reservation, and welcomed me back to our old intimacy. How typical of the woman that was!)

On the last evening of her stay in Jamaica, after George had returned to London, Geraldine lay on the Pumphreys' verandah and accepted a long gin and lime from one of the servants. 'Tell me . . .' she said.

'Yes?' The black face turned instantly to hers.

'Are you happy here?'

'Yes, Miss,' he replied, perhaps fearing that his job might be on the line. 'Mr Pumphrey is a very good employer.'

'And what about other people on the island? Are they happy?'

'Well . . .' said the servant judiciously. 'Some of them are, Miss, and some of them aren't.'

'I see,' said Geraldine. 'Thank you.'

Armed with this research, Geraldine Byers returned to England with a new confidence in her ability to rewrite and continue her Booker Prize-winning novel.

IT'S A FREE COUNTRY
by
G. S. Byers

Just like my sisters. They get invitation to party. I don't get invitation to party. Rain falls, lots of rain splashing in empty tin cans, bouncing off the street, just like back home, only here it soak in, with no sun to dry it out. I don't care. Since I come to England I don't care about myself.

My sisters. I remember days when the rain always come down, dust turn to foaming mud, air damp and hot, but still the mosquitoes bite. I am cooking in the kitchen shed, stirring the mash-up pan, choking in the thick smoke from the wet wood. My father is in the gallery, not thinking about anything as usual, just waiting to eat. And beneath the galvanize roof, my sisters dress up in old sugarsacks, trying to be like star-girls, like Barbara Standick and Rhonda Flem, and waiting to eat. And I am in the kitchen shed doing the cooking.

I know from the rain that it's January, but I don't know the year. In my mind so much happen, I can't say the time it was. All I see is the rain and the yellow mud and the sugarcane and the para-grass and the cooking and the cleaning and my father in the gallery and my sisters dressing up below the galvanize roof and everyone waiting to eat.

I still cook for my sisters. They get invitation to party. The rain stop. Look, through the kitchen window I see wet London buildings. Gutters full of wet rubbish in milky pools, streets clogged and muddy. My sisters go out to shops. They are mockers and jokers. They are happy. And inside me it is heavy.

The man come to read the gas meter. I say things to him I don't mean. 'I'm going to be very successful. I am going to get more money than you have ever seen. I will marry a rich man. I will live in the biggest house in the whole world.'

But even as I talk I know my life spoil. I know my sisters will win through in life. They don't know how jealous I am of them. I know from small how little there is in the world for me.

For my sisters the world is not like that. I know what they do, I see them. When I kill time, they get invitations to parties; when I ride in the donkey-cart, they have cars; when I suck sugarcane, they eat in restaurants. Some people go up in the world and some go down. I go so far down I don't care any more.

My father didn't care. He see my sisters go up in the world and me go down and he don't care. He say he is happy to let things take their own course. He feel that he is very wise to let things take their course. My sisters go away to further their studies. I miss out. My father turns it into a joke. He say I not lose much when I stop school. He say I don't need ambition. He say one day I get married, my husband get drunk and beat me up – that is the old way – I don't need more than that.

But I have ambition and it is always hurting me. I get the ambition for the things I talk about to the man who come to read the gas meter. I want my days to be happy. I want fetes with rum and curry chicken. I want out these rags. I want to dress pretty, so nice and neat like Olivia de Havillam in *Gone With the Wind*. I want to work and work and save and save and have money. I want to marry a professional man who has furthered his studies and has a job in the city. I want no shame.

But I get the shame and it is always hurting. My life ruin. My sisters get invitation to party. I don't get invitation to party. I have no life.

1972

It was in 1972 that Geraldine Byers decided to marry George, and by the end of the year they were wife and man.

I must confess my first reaction to the announcement of their impending marriage was not charitable. Even though I had no right to do so, I did retain an proprietorial interest in George, and I still found myself blaming Geraldine for the ending of our engagement. It was only when she had explained the reasons for their marriage to me in considerable detail that I came to see the error of my attitude.

First, as she patiently spelled out to me, her extensive reading into the literature of feminism, while making her fully aware of the inadequacies of men as a sex, had also brought home to her the limitations, particularly in terms of time-scale, of female physiology. She had read much of biological time-clocks ticking; and a gentle stroll along the King's Road was sufficient to bring home to her that there were certain new fashions for which even she, though an extremely well-preserved thirty-year-old, was now too old. She put this point to me with such charm and clarity that it seemed churlish to mention that I was the victim of identical chronological pressures.

Her second reason for marriage was that the Sunday newspapers printed with increasing frequency scare-mongering articles about the safety of the Pill. Having protected herself with it for over ten years, Geraldine was beginning to think she should either move on to some other form of contraception, or get married and have a go at conception instead.

There was also the undeniable fact that her father had suffered some sort of financial setback in the last year. Though its details remained properly obscure ('not the sort of thing one talks about, old Smartie-tube'), there had apparently been some dealings in a property company, and that property company may have had some distant connection with the 'Poulson affair', which was being distastefully aired in the courts at that time. Though life in Gloucestershire retained its high gloss, Geraldine did once or twice hear her father speaking of economies . . . no, it wasn't as positive as that, but she didn't hear him talking of extravagances with quite his former abandon. There was nothing so crude as a suggestion of reducing her allowance, but she thought it prudent at least to investigate other sources of funding. George, with his considerable inherited wealth and huge salary for whatever it was he did in chemicals, could not be dismissed too lightly from her reckoning.

If this makes Geraldine sound cold-bloodedly mercenary – indeed, that was my first reaction to what she said – the impression is, as I came to realize, false and should be corrected. She was not, as she judiciously reminded me, like other people; she did not just want money for her own ends (her relationship with Mo had taught her the utter unimportance of material things), but she was *a writer*, and, like it or not, she needed money to support her art.

Bursaries from bodies like the Arts Council have always been rare, and yet all writers need some support while their income flickers, gutters and is all too often snuffed out completely. There is no greater inhibition to the fine, ethereal talent of someone like Geraldine Byers than having to think about money all the time. It is therefore only sensible that as many writers as can should try to set up their own alternative domestic Arts Councils to subsidize their genius. Women writers, on the whole, are more successful in making such arrangements than men.

There was, as Geraldine pointed out to me, a long and respectable tradition of patronage in the arts. The talent of Michelangelo might have withered unseen without the backing of Lorenzo de Medici; Mozart's *Cosi fan tutte* been unheard but for the commission of Joseph II of Austria; and would it not therefore be a great kindness if some comparable retrospective lustre were imparted to the name of George for his support of the Booker Prize-winning author, Geraldine Byers?

It was these latter arguments that persuaded me and made me realize how selfish I was being about the whole business. As my friend gently implied, without being so crude as to put the position into words, it was an act of considerable effrontery for me, Mary Mott, a person completely without talent, to advance my claims for anything over those of a genius.

I then understood exactly what she meant and felt rather shame-faced over my behaviour. I asked Geraldine to forgive me; with typical generosity, she consented. As a gesture of pure friendship, she asked me to be a bridesmaid at their wedding. I agreed joyfully.

In fact what finally precipitated Geraldine and George's marriage was not really an argument like those rehearsed above, but an event. Through the early months of 1972, the financial position of *Pivot* had been degenerating faster than ever. Two issues even failed to appear, because the printers refused to undertake further work till their outstanding account was settled. Geraldine tried to keep things going, spreading her net ever wider to find new contributors who didn't know anyone who had written for the magazine and might tip them off about its appalling payment record. But the task was not easy. The resources of stop-gap planning and rearguard action had been stretched as far as they could. Something had to happen.

That something did happen on the night of 17 June. Like the arrest of five men in Washington's Watergate hotel which took place the same night, the happening in the *Pivot* offices made little impression on the media at the time. But both events would have reverberations, one for the future of the American presidency, the other for the future of the Booker Prize.

That afternoon, as Geraldine later recounted to me, Robin Troke-Nuttall returned from lunch nearer five than four, and in a changed mood. He was drunk, certainly, but his drunkenness did not take its usual form of belligerence or stupor; a new, elegiac quality had come into his demeanour. His manner was that of a rather bad amateur Prospero about to break his staff.

'I must get my affairs in order, Geraldine,' he announced with slurred dignity. 'I wasted time, and I must make up that time before time wastes me. Will you please assemble all the outstanding bills and place them on my desk.'

This she did, and hovered in the doorway for further instructions.

Robin Troke-Nuttall looked hazily at the mountain of paper on his desk. 'One quick blitz,' he said carefully, 'and all these could be paid. Then on with the important things in my life. Not too old to salvage something, you know.'

'No,' Geraldine concurred politely. Then, looking at her watch, 'Was there anything else you wanted, Robin?'

His eyes took their time focusing on her. 'Yes, yes, there was.'

'What?'

'I'd like to make love to you, Geraldine.'

'Oh,' she said.

'Always wanted to. Since you started working here.'

'Ah. You never said.'

'No. No, well, doesn't do to say these things. Working relationship, all that.'

'Hmm.'

'Well, what do you say to the idea?'

She wasn't really sure what she said to it. It was not an idea to which she had given any preparatory thought. She didn't fancy Robin Troke-Nuttall, even mildly. On the other hand, she didn't dislike him; and, although she was by then engaged to George, she was a mature, liberated woman, pill-safe to make her own decisions

31

about her life. Above all, she was a writer, and writers have to make themselves open up, tendrils waving hopefully like sea-anemones, to new experiences. Geraldine had never made love with a significantly older man. At the very least, she reckoned, there ought to be a short story in it.

'All right,' she said.

'Ah.' He didn't move. Perhaps he hadn't planned the scenario any further than the initial question.

'When had you in mind?' Geraldine prompted diffidently.

'Well, um . . .' He thought for a moment. 'No time like the present.'

She looked dubiously round the office. 'Where?'

Robin Troke-Nuttall let out a short laugh. 'Rugs in front of gas-fires were traditional scenes of animal passion in my young day.'

'All right,' she said.

The experience – if that word isn't an overstatement – Geraldine described as rather like being crushed by a heavy bolt of tweed. She was aware only of fabric tickling her skin, not of fleshly contact. Overburdened with alcohol, her employer's penis lay slumped between his legs like a drunkard in a gutter. The animal element of his passion was in hibernation.

After about five minutes of imprecise mumbling and fumbling, Robin Troke-Nuttall rolled off her. 'Problem of the creative artist. Always has been. Reconciling the magnificence of the imaginary with the mediocrity of the real.'

Geraldine did not take this personally. As a writer, she knew exactly what he meant. She adjusted her underwear, while Robin rebuttoned his tweeds. He seemed unworried by his failure, even whistled softly to himself. Then he sat at his desk, lit up his pipe and looked over the stack of bills towards her.

'What is it they say at the moment – "Tomorrow is the next day of the rest of my life"?'

Geraldine winced at the cliché, but agreed that it was said.

'Absolutely true. Things to do, Geraldine. Things that are going to be done.'

'Yes.' She hovered again by the door. It was not difficult to imagine that time had been wound backwards, that the last twenty minutes had not happened. 'Was there anything else you wanted, Robin?'

'No, everything fine,' he murmured, already unaware of her. He took a fresh lined pad out of his desk drawer and uncapped his tortoiseshell fountain pen. He looked deeply pensive. Geraldine was in his line of vision, but unseen. She left his office, softly closing the door behind her, and went home.

The next morning, when she arrived for work, the Bloomsbury offices were surrounded by fire engines and police cars. Smoky licks of black rose on the walls above the shattered windows. As with Mo's departure from her emotional life, the decision about when to cut loose from *Pivot* had been made for her.

Robin Troke-Nuttall had perished, roasted like a sucking-pig in flaming tweed. It was not certain whether the fire had been started deliberately or a stray ember had dropped from his pipe on to the pile of bills while he slept. *The Times* gave him a surprisingly full and fulsome obituary; but then there always has been a tradition of mutual back-scratching among Literary Editors.

The future of *Pivot* went up in smoke with its outstanding bills. Only one piece of paper, remarkably, survived the conflagration, protected perhaps by the metal wastebin into which it had been screwed up and thrown.

It was the top sheet of the lined pad on which Robin Troke-Nuttall had been preparing to write when Geraldine left him the night before. On it was written boldly:

'DYLAN THOMAS: THE TRUE REALITY
by Robin Troke-Nuttall.'

The rest of the page was blank.

Geraldine and George had a full traditional white wedding in Gloucestershire at the beginning of November. Geraldine looked magnificent, her slender frame draped in a white designer dress of classical simplicity. I felt I looked less attractive in a rather shapeless dress of peach-coloured brocade. Still, Geraldine had chosen the bridesmaids' dresses, and it was her day, after all.

Anyway, I had nothing to complain about. With characteristic generosity, it was to me that Geraldine threw her bouquet!

Mo had been invited to the wedding 'for old times' sake' and surprised everyone by accepting the invitation. He surprised them more by appearing in full morning dress with relatively short hair and neat Zapata moustache.

Mr Byers had pulled out all the stops for the occasion ('only the best for you, my little bread-and-butter-pudding'), but was seen to wince more than once at some of the bills that came in. This gave Geraldine a feeling of vindication for the timing of her move to alternative arts funding.

The young couple – well, *fairly* young – were to honeymoon in Rome. Geraldine 'went away' in a Ginger Group suit with broad straight trousers and huge buttons on the smock-like jacket. George wore a shaggy sheepskin coat she had bought for him. At that stage Geraldine still believed that she could reconstitute her husband's sartorial image along with all the other elements of his character which she proposed to change. She wanted to get him away from the 'Mr Suit' persona. But the sheepskin looked incongruous. Gradually, reluctantly, over the ensuing years, Geraldine was to come to realize what I could have told her from the start – that George had actually been designed to wear suits; he didn't look right in anything else.

Because of the timing of the honeymoon, they were away for the announcement of the Booker Prize winner, so they only heard of John Berger's bizarre attack on its sponsors and intention to share the money with the Black Panthers after their return. But the prize was not forgotten in Rome. Geraldine had packed all four shortlisted novels and, in the interludes between sight-seeing, eating and (she told me afterwards with relish) very good sex, she read religiously through John Berger, Susan Hill, Thomas Keneally and David Storey.

She even started work on her proposed intellectual reorganization of her husband by getting George to read some of the books. But it wasn't easy; he didn't have the habit of reading, and some of his reactions were embarrassingly simplistic. Half-way through John Berger's *G*, for example, he apparently put the book down and announced, 'I've never read such a load of pretentious cobblers.'

'Really!' Geraldine hastened to silence him. 'You mustn't say that. John Berger is an enormously important art critic.'

'That may be so,' George countered stoutly, 'but he's a lousy novelist.'

'No, no. It's just that you don't understand him.'

'Not sure that I want to. He seems to be telling about half a dozen stories at the same time and just when one of them gets interesting, he stops and starts talking about how inadequate words are to describe things.'

'Of course,' said Geraldine, as if speaking to a five-year-old child. 'That is *exactly* the point he's making.'

'Well, I'm sorry. It still seems like codswallop to me.'

At that point, Geraldine confessed to me, she did for a moment wonder whether the marriage had been a mistake. Her husband's intellectual reconstruction was clearly going to take longer than she had originally estimated. Why on earth had someone of her artistic sensibility allied herself to someone so unbelievably crass?

But later that night, as he brought her to new heights of overlapping ecstasy in their hotel room, the question seemed less important.

She returned from honeymoon with her creative batteries recharged, ready for the challenge of a totally new approach to the Booker Book.

*

C
by
Geraldine Byers

O

The uncle of the secondary protagonist of this book was called Alberto. He was a king from an Italian city. He was a tall thin man who looked short because of the size of his crown.

I cannot continue this account of the uncle of the secondary protagonist of this book. Sequential narrative and the convergence of plotting towards a conclusion are fatal to writers. Conclusions conclude. Ending is always the easy way out.

When Lucrezia was a small child she realized the profound differences of a woman's body which set her apart from men. As she grew up the hair-trigger reactions of its secret aspects became more precious to her and she was glad of this.

La donna e mobile.

On 11 May 1860 Garibaldi and 'the thousand heroes' landed at Marsala.

Garibaldi became a folk hero.

After Garibaldi's death, throughout Italy streets and piazzas were named after him.

Not to mention biscuits.

O

How did it happen that on 15 December 1904, Lucrezia sat in her bedroom, brushing her hair with a tortoiseshell brush, dressed only in thin linen shift?

When the boy came to see her she said: how beautiful the geraniums are for the time of year. Then she asked him to go and check that the wheels had been replaced on the hay-wain. After he had gone, she thought: well, I never.

POEM FOR LUCREZIA
Intermittently my shape alters
Unlike the fixed outlines of a photograph
Noise has no admittance

Into the ferocious stillness of my hair
The cutting of my toenails is articulate
Their shavings retained
I stay where I stand
My hands are at the end of my arms
Like
Like the ferocious stillness of my hair.

THE CONGO

The Congo used to be a little-known country of Lower Guinea, W. Africa, separated from Loango on the N. by the Congo, and bounded on the S. by Angola. The soil on the banks of the river is fertile, but the climate is intensely hot.

Lucrezia must be thirty-five. Her hair spreads loose over her shoulders. A geranium stands in a pot on her bedside table. Its smell is pervasively real.

The boy comes in and tells her he has checked the spokes on the hay-wain. They are all where they should be.

Lucrezia reaches out towards him.

He moves forward towards her.

They roar with laughter.

And who can blame them?

Beneath her shift Lucrezia is soft and hard (like an apricot) and soft and soft (like a feather pillow). She looms beneath him, uninterruptedly huge.

Her breasts predicate his maturity.

Without hesitation, he puts his hand on her mythology. She opens to enclose his finger.

His penis finds the labyrinth of her obscurity.

He is absorbed.

The softness.

Ooh.

Aah.

Previously, it was unrealized, a poem hovering, waiting to be written.

Now it isn't.

O

C. was full of sexual desire, but he had not yet found the proper outlet for that desire.

He had followed the lodestone of his penis to the furthest poles of experience.

But without success.

Which was why he decided to invite a lot of women to a party, in the hope of finding the right one.

Or having a good time, anyway.

O

Sexual desire is by its nature targeted. It can be generalized or focused on an individual. It can be focused on one part of an individual. A breast, a cunt, in some instances an elbow.

In a disordered unco-ordinated world sexual desire can be a bonding factor: with her, life will be easier and there'll be someone to do the shopping.

In a formalized structured world sexual desire is compounded by a random unpredictablity: cor, I wouldn't half mind a bit of that.

Why does writing about sexual experience, despite the imprecision of all such attempts, become such an integral part of much literature?

First, because in the recesses of the human mind the void between sexual desire and sexual fulfilment is perhaps one of the most relevant expressions of the creative artist's difficulties in reconciling the architectural plans of his imagination with the dry bricks of reality which must be used to build those edifices.

And, second, because people like books with a bit of sex in them.

Which means they're more likely to buy them.

I make two crude drawings:

Why?

Because people are more likely to buy impenetrable books if they have smutty pictures in them.

O

Giddy-up!

The wood was still. The trees stood unmoving in their trunks. The soft mulch of leaves lay incommunicative on the ground.

Giddy-up!

The boy's cry sounds like an empty oil-drum being beaten with a damp French loaf.

Giddy-up!

The dog answers it unwillingly. The boy realizes that his invasion of nature has bestowed a kind of maturity on him.

O

Some say my writing drowns in its own superfluity; that the constant shifting in style and metaphor have the end result that none of it means anything. Well, they may have a point.

Forests do not have political convictions. Nor do mountains.

Nor do penises, come to that.

They are all sublimely tolerant of anything that happens.

A bit like readers, I hope.

1973

It was in 1973 that Geraldine had the brilliant idea of my writing her biography. Sensitive as ever, with that compassion which is the distinguishing mark of greatness, she had observed that I still felt a little hurt by her marriage to George and thoughtfully hastened to provide a project which would fill the void he had left in my life.

She proposed the idea one evening when George was away and I had dropped round to their Holland Park house to cook supper for her. I was so surprised that at first I could not think how to respond. I had recently started a new job as office manager for a firm of solicitors, and I wasn't sure that I had time to take on anything else. However, Geraldine made clear to me just what an opportunity I was being offered, and gave me such strong assurances of her co-operation that I could not refuse her. She even agreed to record all of her telephone calls from the house and give me the tapes to transcribe, so that I could bring greater verisimilitude to my narrative. I don't think there ever was a biographer who was so willingly vouchsafed so much research material!

The phone rang for a full two minutes before an accusatory voice answered, 'Abrams & Willis.'

'Oh, hello. My name's Geraldine Byers.' She left a little half-beat pause, but the accusatory voice didn't say, 'What – Geraldine Byers, the author of that enchanting book, *Pale Cast of Thought*?', so she went on, 'Could I speak to Sidney Parrott, please?'

'What is it in connection with?' The accusatory voice now sounded as if it was on the verge of extracting a full confession.

'I'm one of Sidney's authors.'

'Oh?'

Clearly that wasn't sufficient recommendation. 'I wrote *Pale Cast of Thought*.'

'Did you?' This was apparently no recommendation at all, but finally, grudgingly, and without much hope, the voice said, 'Well, I'll try putting you through.'

Apparently against the odds, Sidney was in his office. 'Hello?' he said, very defensive. Perhaps he had recently been given the third degree by the girl on the switchboard.

'Hello, Sidney. It's Geraldine.'

'Ah. How nice.' But his voice was still cautious, waiting for clues as to which of a whole telephone directory of Geraldines this one might be.

'Geraldine Byers.'

'Of course.' He became even more defensive. 'Haven't had the absolutely most recent figures yet, but the last lot of sales were well . . . weren't they?'

Perhaps the word he was looking for was 'terrible'. 'Appalling' would have done. 'Non-existent' might actually have been nearer the mark, because *Pale Cast of Thought* had been out of print for some years.

'Quite encouraging,' Sidney Parrott said finally, and inaccurately.

'I wasn't ringing about *Pale Cast of Thought*,' said Geraldine.

'Ah.' Now he sounded positively paranoid, and leapt instantly to his traditional defence in all circumstances. 'Look, let's have lunch and talk about it.'

They met in the almost peasant simplicity of Bertorelli's in Charlotte Street. According to Geraldine, Sidney Parrott always lunched people there. The restaurant's familiarity perhaps gave a boost to his confidence, though from the anxious way his eyes were darting about when she entered, it was apparently not much of a boost. He rose to greet her, brushing breadcrumbs off his striped suit, adjusting his bow-tie and straightening his glasses before he shook her hand.

'Lovely to see you,' he said vaguely, 'lovely. Been so long.'

There was some confusion between Sidney and the waiter over hanging up her knitted maxi-coat, but once that task had been achieved and they were seated, he asked if she'd like anything to drink 'apart from wine?' This enquiry, accompanied by a gesture to the bottle of red in front of him, was an example of what Latin masters used to describe as 'a question expecting the answer No'.

Geraldine said wine was fine, and he splashed some liberally over the area of white tablecloth where her glass stood.

'Cheers,' he said, raising his own. 'Terrible business, all this, isn't it?'

'What?'

Her question threw him. 'Well, um, I mean the whole thing. All this three-day week business and, you know, the power restrictions and . . . well, you know. Walking round London after dark, you'd think you were back in the Blitz.'

'Oh yes.' Geraldine took no interest in politics – at that stage of her life she feared that her creativity could only be coarsened by too much contact with reality – but even she could not be unaware of the effects that December of Edward Heath's test of strength against the miners.

'Dreadful,' Sidney continued. 'Trying to do some Christmas shopping last week, couldn't get into the spirit at all. Bloody Arabs.'

'No. Of course we have been spoiled by having cheap fossil fuel for a very long time.' Since the conversation had taken this tedious turn, Geraldine decided she might as well quote George verbatim.

'Oh yes.'

'And the Stock Market doesn't look too healthy either.' Her father had lost a packet on shares earlier that month following the withdrawal of Arab funds from London.

'And inflation . . .' Sidney didn't feel he needed to do more than shrug after saying the word.

'Mm,' Geraldine commiserated. 'Is it all having an effect in publishing?'

Sidney, who had begun to relax a little, was instantly on the defensive again. 'What? Oh yes, I'll say. Inevitably, really. Lists'll be cut back . . . bound to be some redundancies. Afraid some of the smaller houses may go to the wall.'

'But Abrams & Willis'll be all right . . . ?' asked Geraldine with a grin.

'Still there at the moment . . .' Sidney replied cautiously, 'though they're talking about all kinds of worrying things . . . you know, really marketing books hard, like packets of detergents.'

'Oh dear.'

'Reducing the numbers of staff . . .'

'How ghastly.'

'Even been some nasty mutterings about cutting back on publication of books that don't sell,' he continued bravely.

'Good heavens.'

'I know, it's a dreadful idea.' He hastily tried to cover up his insensitive introduction of the subject. 'I mean, you know and I know that one should publish because one believes in a book, not because of the number of copies it's going to sell. Some of our best authors have never made any profits at all for us, but we're still damned proud to have published them. And, anyway, it's only through our encouraging talent by publishing early stuff which doesn't sell that writers get the chance to write their successful books.'

'Yes.'

'Mind you,' he said reflectively, 'just when they do get to the successful ones, they have a nasty habit of moving on to other publishers.'

'Oh dear.'

'Happened quite a lot recently. There's a nasty sort of barrow-boy mentality creeping into the world of publishing. I mean, obviously not so much the established publishers themselves . . .'

'No, of course not. Publishing still the last refuge of a gentleman?'

He straightened his bow-tie diffidently. 'One likes to think so. No, I was talking more of . . . what do they call them? Marketing people? And of course . . .' He winced as he approached the word, 'Agents.'

'Ah.'

'You don't have an agent, do you, Geraldine my dear?'

'No.'

'Keep it that way. Nothing an agent can do for you that can't be done by a conscientious publisher.' He mopped up the last juices from his *saltimbocca alla romana* with a piece of bread and sat back for his set-piece. 'I always think the relationship between publisher and author should be like a marriage, two people who want to be together on a one-to-one basis, each wishing the best for the other, each trying to help. Well, you don't want a third party in a marriage, do you?'

'No,' Geraldine agreed devoutly.

'Otherwise publishing becomes just such a sordid, commercial transaction. You lose the . . . well, I can only call it the *love* of books, which is what should send someone into publishing in the first place.'

'Yes,' Geraldine agreed equally devoutly.

'But some of the new breed in the business . . .' Sidney shook his head, then flicked his fingers for more wine, as if to take his mind off the distasteful matters of which he spoke. However, the subject wouldn't go away so easily. 'I mean, what they're doing are not *books*. Not *books* in the real sense. Oh, they've got pages and words in them, but, really, is something which is completely based on a television series a *book*? Is a memoir of some superannuated film-star a *book*?'

Geraldine shook her head at the appropriate moments.

'No, of course they're not,' said Sidney, his hobby-horse rearing up magnificently. 'But the distressing thing is – they sell. And that's all some of the new breed of oiks who've come into publishing care about. I mean . . .' His hands flapped as he searched for an example. 'Do you know Maurice Ashby of P & L Books?'

'Well . . .' Geraldine replied cautiously.

'Used to be called Peace and Love Books.'

'Oh yes.'

'Well, he's into all this celebrity publishing nonsense. Disgusting, I call it.'

'But wouldn't you say . . .' Geraldine began, feeling that perhaps she owed Mo some defence for the years they had spent together, 'wouldn't you say that publishing that kind of book is a valid way of supporting the less commercially viable side of a list?'

'Oh, I don't think so, no. Publishers shouldn't think about the commercial side; all they should think about is books. Good books and bad books. They should reject the bad books, and print the good ones – that's what publishing should be about.'

'Hm.'

'But, oh no, all the new lot think about is money. Money, money and more money. Offering large advances to poach successful authors from other houses – I think that's just not on.'

'No, of course not.'

'But authors fall for it every time. The oldest trick in the book.'

'Don't you think,' Geraldine posited tentatively, 'that a professional author has a kind of duty to make as much from his or her writing as possible . . . ?'

'No,' said Sidney. 'A professional author has a duty to his or her talent, and to his or her publisher. Those should be the most important considerations.'

'Mm.'

'But,' he continued with a lugubrious shake of his head, 'you try and tell them that. Some authors are very irresponsible.'

Geraldine flashed him her most charming smile. 'I hope I don't come under that blanket condemnation.'

'Oh, good Lord no,' he hastened to assure her. 'No, you've been very loyal. We've published all your stuff, haven't we?'

'Yes. Of course, there has only been the one book so far.'

'Has there?' He recovered the ground quickly. 'Oh yes, yes, of course there has. And what a fine book it was.'

'Thank you.'

'Very fine. No, I'll always remember that authentic *frisson* of delight I felt when I first read . . . um . . . um . . .' His eyes blinked in desperate ignorance from behind his glasses.

'*Pale Cast of Thought*,' Geraldine supplied.

'Exactly. Exactly. *Pale Cast of Thought*. Wonderful, wonderful. I was always slightly disappointed it didn't make a bigger impact on publication. Thought it might have sold a few more, but . . . well, better a *succès d'estime* than . . . er . . .'

'Yes. Sidney, there was one thing I wanted to ask you.'

His defences were instantly up. 'If it's about precise sales figures, I'm sorry, but it's very difficult for me to get that kind of information.'

'No, no, it wasn't about that.'

Sidney Parrott relaxed visibly. 'What then, my dear?'

'It's about the new book I'm writing.'

'Oh. You're writing a new book?' This didn't sound like the most welcome news he had received that year.

'Yes. I've been working on it on and off for three or four years . . .'

'Uh-uh.'

'And I think I've only now really homed in on the right style for it.'

'Ah.'

'Have you read *The Siege of Krishnapur*?'

He looked blank. 'No. I don't think we published that, did we?'

'No, no, you didn't. It was Weidenfeld & Nicolson.'

'Oh, well then . . .' Sidney Parrott shrugged, his ignorance vindicated. He couldn't be expected to keep up with what other houses were publishing.

'It's by J. G. Farrell.'

He shook his head. The name meant nothing.

'Just won the Booker Prize.'

Another shrug. That meant nothing, either.

'Anyway, my new book's rather in that style. I think it could be very successful.'

'Oh, really? Well, maybe. And how far have you got with the book?'

'Only a few chapters.'

This information seemed to reassure him. 'Jolly good show. Well, you keep at it, lots of luck, and when it's finished, I'd be delighted to cast an eye over it. Hope it gives me as much of a thrill as . . . um . . . um . . .'

'*Pale Cast of Thought*.'

'*Pale Cast of Thought*, exactly.'

Sidney Parrott sat back in relief. The business part of the lunch was, he felt confident, concluded. 'Now, shall we investigate the sweets . . . ?'

'The thing is . . .' Geraldine began.

'Yes, my dear?'

'I'm finding the book a bit difficult . . .'

'Ah well,' he said urbanely, 'I'm afraid writing books is a difficult business.'

'And I thought, since you're my editor . . .'

'Hm?'

'Maybe you'd have a look at what I've written so far and give me your thoughts . . . ?'

'What, you mean *read* it?' asked Sidney Parrott.

'Yes. Yes, please.'

'Oh.' Geraldine described to me with her customary vividness the desperation in his eye as her editor looked round the restaurant for excuses, and I was as relieved as she was to hear that he could not come up with any. 'Oh, very well,' he agreed grudgingly. 'I'll read it.'

THE BALL OF CALCUTTA
by
G. S. Byers

5

The Collector, Mr Hardy, was held in high esteem by the European community; no doubt this was because none of them knew him well. He was a man of becoming gravity, with an exact, though occasionally inaccurate, sense of social proprieties. His first wife had died during the hot weather her first summer in Krishnapur, leaving him with a small daughter. Obedient to the obligations of his race and calling, the Collector had made it his business to remarry at the earliest opportunity; though it was said by some in Government circles that his selection had been dictated more by haste than discrimination. The second Mrs Hardy suffered from a condition little esteemed in Indian society; she was 'country born' and had therefore never been to England. Added to this impediment, she was a widow and, though some widows brought a welcome sparkle to the expatriate community, the second Mrs Hardy seemed to bring little more than the lumber of two daughters. These girls were plump and unsuited to the exigencies of the Indian climate; both perspired far too freely, and no amount of rice powder was sufficient to eradicate the sheen from their features; both, also, were frequent martyrs to 'prickly heat'.

The Collector, though increasingly obsessed by a sense of impending doom and an urgency to return to Krishnapur to take up his duties, was determined to waste no opportunities during the cold season in Calcutta. He was fully aware of the obligations placed upon him by his second marriage, and was tireless in his search for young officers incautious or myopic enough to take on the responsibility of his two stepdaughters. His sense of propriety would not allow him to enter his own daughter into the matrimonial lists until he had done his duty by her stepsisters, and, since his second wife seemed to have affected a permanent indisposition, he set out grimly to fulfill his parental obligations unassisted.

He became a familiar figure as the weather grew hotter in Calcutta, riding in a *gharry* through the scorching heat of the middle of the day, on his way to pay calls on various dignitaries who might further the progress of his quest. He was regularly to be seen in the drawing-rooms of unmarried officers' mammas; frequently drinking with their fathers in the Bengal Club; or attending meetings at the racecourse, earwigging for the first news of imminent balls or the arrivals of new officers. There was nothing, the Collector calculated, like the disorientation following five interminable months at sea, so liable to precipitate a young lieutenant into ruining his career by a disastrous marriage.

Lieutenant Charman was recently arrived from England and would shortly be joining the 15th at Berhampur. He was eagerly caught up in the last weeks of the Season, which that year had been unusually successful. His presence was avidly sought at balls, weddings and other entertainments. He endeared himself to the masculine society of Calcutta by his prowess at pig-sticking. At the running of the Bengal Club Cup, ambitious mammas with unmarried daughters were so busy casting covetous eyes on him that some did not see the horses at all. And the novelty of his presence quickly erased any initial impression that he might be rather fat. Arriving so near the end of the cold season, he was just the sort of new face to reanimate jaded Calcutta drawing-rooms. Besides, his father was known to be a Director, which guaranteed social eminence in the Company's India. The rumour that the Lieutenant had been clapped on the back by Lord Canning within an hour of his arrival may well have been apocryphal, but it was a measure of the young man's stature that such myths should gather around him. No wonder the intelligence of his presence in Calcutta caused considerable flutterings in the Hardys' house in Alipore.

The news that Lieutenant Charman was to attend the last ball of the cold season in the town hall brought these flutterings to a level matched only by humming-birds. The two elder Miss Hardys (they had taken the Collector's name at the time of his marriage to their mother) immediately summoned their dressmakers, and *gharries* crisscrossed Calcutta with great frequency, bearing bolts of silk, crinoline hoops and petticoats, together with a selection of white satin shoes. The Collector stroked his side-whiskers dourly and grumbled about the expense of new dresses so late in the Season, but could not help admitting the strength of his stepdaughters' arguments. One *galloppe* with Lieutenant Charman would certainly justify the investment. As he looked dispassionately at his stepdaughters, the Collector tried to convince himself that the night of the ball would be unaccountably cool, that sufficient rice powder could wreak miracles, that the lighting might be dim in the town hall, or that Lieutenant Charman might prove to be deeply stupid.

1974

(What follows is a reconstruction of a major crisis in the life of a creative artist. It is almost impossible for someone like me, Mary Mott, who has never experienced the torments of genius, to empathize fully with a true writer's sufferings, and if the ensuing account even approximates to the reality, it is thanks to Geraldine Byers' selfless willingness to talk to me in great depth about the agonies she endured in 1974.)

It was a perfect autumn day, no wind, the veld stretched palely away to the horizon, the drought was unbroken.

Geraldine sighed and looked out of the window, past the Laura Ashley curtains, through the buildings to the tips of the leafless trees in Holland Park. God, it was hell being a writer.

She contemplated making another cup of coffee, but knew she must ration her breaks; her day, like her prose style, would become too jerky and staccato if overpunctuated. She wondered if she was feeling cold. In a draught, maybe? Or just cold – it was December, after all. But she had only just sat down after turning up the central heating and checking the double glazing on the windows. She couldn't really still feel cold; she didn't really need to go and get another jumper to put on over her denim dungarees. No, she was just making excuses.

Anyway, now she came to think of it, she felt too hot rather than too cold. Perhaps she'd overdone turning up the heating, perhaps she should go and wind the control down again, perhaps she should —

But no. That would be just more procrastination. She was a writer. It was her job to write. When the inspiration wasn't there, it was part of the mystery of her God-given talent to be able to conjure up the demons of creativity. She brought the green Venus 2B pencil firmly down to the page of her orange-covered feint-ruled school exercise book. She would write something. She would write her way back into creative flow. She scored through what she had already written.

After a quarter of an hour she assessed the new opening sentence.

No wind, the veld stretched palely away to the horizon, the drought was unbroken, it was a perfect autumn day.

47

She still didn't feel convinced by it. She looked round the room, decorated in the required Laura Ashley cowshed style, and indulged in that common habit of writers: blaming the surroundings.

She wondered, not for the first time, whether Holland Park was the right place for a novelist to give of her best. Was she really writing as well now as she used to do in Notting Hill? It was only a few hundred yards up the road geographically, but in spiritual terms, what a huge chasm there now seemed to be between her old fluency and this new creative constipation.

Maybe she needed to get away from everything. A cottage in Cornwall, perhaps? Scotland? Ireland? Somewhere where the harsh sounds of the city would be stilled and she could listen only to the uninterrupted promptings of her muse. But could she cope with that kind of isolation? Probably not, she decided. Writing was, as she still insisted on telling anyone who raised the subject, a lonely life, and to add physical isolation to the spiritual isolation of the artist could only make the loneliness worse. She needed the stimulus of other intellects. Married to George, she sometimes thought the conversation of her literary friends was the only thing that kept her going.

So that meant, by definition, that she had to work in London. But was Holland Park the right part of London? Did the mix of people there mulch down into a suitable compost for the nourishment of her deep-rooted talent? There were a few writers and other artists about, but there were also bankers, solicitors, barristers, surgeons, stockbrokers and people in dreary things like chemicals. Perhaps they didn't really offer enough intellectual stimulus for a fine mind like Geraldine's. No, she must talk to George about it soon. There were no two ways about it – they would have to move to Hampstead.

She dragged her attention back to the page, scribbled through her latest draft, and grafted on for another twenty minutes.

The veld stretched palely away to the horizon, the drought was unbroken, it was a perfect autumn day, no wind.

She wasn't sure that this was an improvement, and scratched the sentence out in a fit of pique.

A pale cast of thought shadowed her mind, reminding her of the ability she had once had as a writer. Surely she'd been less self-conscious during the composition of her first and only completed novel. Yes, then her imagination had been like a young colt, bursting through curbs and restraints, eager to score its bold hoofmarks across the virgin prairie of her feint-ruled pages.

For a second, she wondered whether that image was good enough to note down, but decided against it.

Anyway, the pale cast of thought that darkened her mind was not just the melancholy remembrance of things past; it also cast its ominous shadow over her future, over her whole *raison d'être* as a writer. Not for the first time – it had happened with increasing frequency in recent months – she wondered about the direction of her creative life. Was she really doing the right thing in devoting her undoubted talent so single-mindedly towards the chimera of a Booker Prize win?

She knew it was heresy, she knew it threatened everything she believed in as an artist, but the thought niggled away at her, corrupting her mind with self-doubt. She tried to argue against it. Circumstances were against her; her destined mission had not been helped that year by the Booker Prize being divided between two authors. Nadine Gordimer's *The Conservationist* and Stanley Middleton's *Holiday* had won it jointly, but Geraldine had never been in any doubt as to which one she should use as her model. Middleton's book was set in the North of England, so there was really no contest. Geraldine, who had never been North of Gloucestershire – except of course for fishing holidays in Scotland, but then Scotland didn't count – knew she would find it a lot easier to enter the mind of a South African than of someone from that unknown area of England, with its jumble of contiguous towns – Birmingham, Leeds, Liverpool, Hull, Bradford, Manchester, Carlisle, Sheffield, Newcastle and so on – where people with flat caps talked with flattened vowels.

So it has had to be the Gordimer. Not easy, though. So much effort in the choice of every word, no sentence allowed to be simple and unadorned. Geraldine looked again at her own latest scored-out effort, and wondered for a moment whether she should change her manner of composition. Some writers of her acquaintance claimed to write the bit that came easiest first, and derided her sequential, story-telling approach. It might be worth trying, she mused. Maybe she should move straight on to the gratuitous sex scene, in which her protagonist was to stick his finger up an unknown girl beside him in an aeroplane. That might flow a bit more easily.

No. She had her standards. She had always written sequentially, grinding out the agony of a complete first draft, rewriting every sentence punctiliously along the way. For Geraldine Byers, as she often said to people who asked about her working methods (and almost as often to people who didn't), writing was like sculpture. Her first draft was simply the block of marble from which her final *oeuvre* had painstakingly to be chipped. Unfortunately, she would then say with a wry smile, we writers cannot just have our block of marble delivered ready from the quarry; we have the additional burden of creating our own medium.

(It was of course a source of great chagrin to her that, since the completion of *Pale Cast of Thought* and since her creative life had been so religiously targeted on the Booker Prize, she hadn't had the chance to finish one of her blocks of marble or begin on the chipping process.)

God, it's hell being a writer, she thought again, gritting her teeth and summoning up her last resources of determination to readdress the sentence in her orange-coloured exercise book. She toiled away for half an hour this time.

> The drought was unbroken, it was a perfect autumn day, no wind, the veld stretched palely away to the horizon.

It was no good. Now she had to face the truth. She tore out the feint-ruled sheet, screwed it up and hurled it towards her rather attractive Laura Ashley wastepaper basket. It missed, echoing in unnatural pathetic fallacy, she thought, her own life.

Geraldine Byers was suffering from Writer's Block.

She turned this idea over in her mind, relishing its sweet pain. As her body seemed to be, in spite of George's regular and assiduous attentions, so her mind was sterile. The creative juices had dried up.

She was not the first to have suffered this agony, she told herself tragically, nor would she be the last, but each writer must suffer pain alone. It was a burden that writers bore, a curse. Yes, she thought, warming to the image, it was a kind of literary menstruation, a pain that must be borne as part of the creative cycle; nothing can be produced without it.

She raised her green Venus 2B pencil to make a note of this rather clever metaphor, certain she could use it somewhere, but stopped herself. She was creatively sterile, after all; it wouldn't do to compromise the perfection of that sterility by having a good idea.

She sat back, almost relaxed, now that she had faced the worst. Like someone who has finally had her cancer confirmed, she knew that she must husband her dwindling energy, that little could now be expected of her. A cure for her condition might be possible, but it would be a slow process; rehabilitation to anything like her former creative persona was a distant prospect. In the short-term, all she could do was try to reconcile herself to her tragic situation.

And tell as many people about it as possible.

I was privileged to be one of the first people she rang. Though I was in the middle of something of a work crisis at the solicitors', I listened to her sufferings for twenty minutes and hope I was properly sympathetic.

50

When she had finished talking to me, Geraldine reached again for the phone, and fixed to meet her friend, Virginia Rawson, for lunch.

Virginia Rawson was a writer, too. Geraldine did not tarnish the purity of her acquaintance by mixing with people who weren't connected with the arts (except for George and me, of course).

But Geraldine always felt at ease with Virginia because her friend was so much a lesser writer than she was herself. Not lesser in terms of productivity; Virginia Rawson was always churning the stuff out; indeed, she might almost have earned the dismissive epithet, 'prolific'. It was what she wrote, however, that put her so much further down the literary pecking order than Geraldine Byers. She was a writer of crime novels, so obviously, since her only aim was to entertain by producing rather well-written stories which people enjoyed reading, Virginia Rawson couldn't be taken too seriously by the literary establishment.

The difference between them was never actually vocalized, but was something of which Geraldine was constantly aware, and she found it imparted a kind of calm to their encounters. It removed the competitive element, which is unfortunately all too common when two writers meet. Since there was no artistic comparison between their work, the issue of relative merit never arose. And, because the only arguments Virginia could raise to support the value of the stuff she wrote were enthusiastic reviews and large international sales, these things were never mentioned. Geraldine thought of Virginia as one of her dearest friends.

Virginia Rawson was unmarried and, as Geraldine once expressed it to me with characteristic benevolence, probably quite attractive to the sort of man who goes for a good figure, sparkling eye, outgoing manner and ready wit. Virginia rarely seemed to have a man on the scene, though; she did spend a great deal of time on her little books and perhaps, Geraldine surmised, that didn't leave room for a love-life. This was probably just as well, because it meant that Virginia could always give absolutely undivided attention to the emotional or creative problems of her friend.

In the matter of the new and tragic Writer's Block, however, as Geraldine reported to me after their meeting, Virginia did not manifest as much sympathy as she should have done.

'Oh yes, it's a pig, isn't it?' was all she said after the dramatic pronouncement had been made.

'You mean, you too have suffered?' Geraldine tried not to feel her anguish diminished by this matter-of-fact reaction, but it did nonetheless seem cheapened in some way. Surely you couldn't get *proper* Writer's Block over the sort of stuff Virginia wrote?

'Keeps happening to me, yes. What people *call* Writer's Block.'

'What do you mean, Virginia? It *is* Writer's Block.'

'What are the symptoms?'

'I . . . can't . . . write,' Geraldine murmured tragically.

'Can't get the words down on paper, don't seem to have any ideas, hate what you've written so far, hate the thoughts you've got for the rest of what you're going to write?'

'Yes, those are . . . some of the symptoms,' Geraldine conceded.

'Well, it's caused by one of two things. Either you're just mentally exhausted . . .'

Geraldine sighed painfully. 'Well, that is possible . . . I'm afraid I do tend to push myself very hard when I'm — '

'Or,' Virginia went on, 'you just haven't done enough planning.'

'What?'

'Got to do the groundwork before you start, haven't you?'

'Yes, but — '

'What's the background of this book you're working on?'

'Well, it's South Africa, but — '

'Have you ever been to South Africa?'

'No, but Daddy has always had a lot of business acquaintances there, so I've met people who — '

'You can't expect to write about somewhere unless you do some research.'

'I've read some books,' Geraldine protested righteously.

'Clearly not enough.' Geraldine had forgotten how inconsiderately brusque Virginia's manner could be at times. 'Look, Geraldine love, you know you can only write about what you know about . . .'

'Well . . .'

'Or what you've researched in proper detail.'

'I always find,' Geraldine said magnificently, 'that too much research inhibits my creative flow. I mean,' she continued, finding a contemporary example which might coincidentally put Virginia's category of fiction firmly in its place, 'it's not as if I want to turn into some kind of Frederick Forsyth, is it?'

'You could learn a lot from reading him. Not about character, but about research and plotting. Have you read *The Day of the Jackal*?'

Geraldine winced. 'Good heavens, no. George has, but — '

'And he enjoyed it.'

'Yes, he did, but . . . I'm not sure that that's a recommendation.'

Virginia grinned. 'Sometimes, you know, Geraldine, you are the most unbelievable intellectual snob.'

'What?' Geraldine felt tears prickling behind her eyes. 'Virginia, I'm going through a very difficult time. I think of you as a friend, and I don't find it very helpful if you just insult me and make me feel worse.'

Virginia's hand enclosed hers across the table. 'Don't worry about it, love. You'll be fine. Just two things you've got to remember . . .'

Geraldine sniffed. 'What?'

'First, don't take yourself too seriously.'

Huh, what a trivial catchpenny platitude, thought Geraldine, who knew that it was impossible for a creative artist of her calibre to take herself too seriously.

'And, second, bear in mind something G. K. Chesteron said . . .'

Why was it Virginia's examples and quotations were always drawn from the second rank of literature? It must be the old truism that it takes one to know one, Geraldine concluded.

'What did he say?' she asked with a magnanimous smile.

' "The artistic temperament is a disease that afflicts amateurs." '

Geraldine sometimes wondered whether Virginia was actually such a good friend, after all.

She took her tragic condition home with her and spent another hour on the phone to me about it. This was a little inconvenient, because my work crisis of that morning had not gone away, but I realized the importance of supporting my gifted friend in her hour of need. Since she was too exhausted and fraught to cope with domestic arrangements, I agreed to cancel my opera seats for that evening and go round to cook a meal for her and George.

So I was there when she told George about the dreadful thing that had happened that morning. He was properly surprised that Virginia hadn't been more understanding; he had always found her the most sympathetic of his wife's friends; no doubt, Geraldine had long since decided, because she wrote the kind of stuff that even his intellect could cope with. He himself was very solicitous and asked if there was anything he could do to help.

Geraldine knew her husband better than to hope for creative empathy, but while his soul remained empty, his wallet was always full, and so she said she needed a complete break. She had to get away from the pressures of her work, to have time to think, time to reconstruct her shattered genius. Thank goodness, whatever her emotional state, Geraldine always had the good sense to recognize when the fragile apparatus of her mind was over-stretched. I would not like to be chronicling posthumously the life of another Virginia Woolf!

So she and George spent Christmas in an expensive hotel in York. They ate a lot, drank a lot, and George's love-making maintained its customary high standard.

But, more important than all that for her development as an artist, Geraldine was in the North. She heard waiters and shopkeepers and sightseers in the Minster all talking with northern accents as if it were the most natural thing in the world. When George drove her up into the Dales, she saw something that she thought might have been a mine. She felt herself assimilating the reality of the North.

On her return to Holland Park, refreshed, invigorated and with her creative energies restored, she burnt the orange-covered school exercise book that contained her attempts at Nadine Gordimer. No, for once she would follow Virginia's advice. She would write about what she knew about. She settled down to reread Stanley Middleton's *Holiday*.

TIME OFF
by
Geraldine Byers
7

After breakfast next morning Edmund Button left his digs for a walk on the promenade.

His father had always taken him for a walk, a gaze out at the sea and a few invigorating breaths of the ozone. The pair would stop in the newsagent for a newspaper. His father'd point to the inch-high headlines of the picture-daily and pass some comment on the idiocy of folk. His moustache bristled as he pontificated, amiable, blustering, haranguing. 'Up to no good, any of 'em, I sh'd think.' When Albert Button passed a comment, the whole world was his audience.

This morning the waves banked gently, pushing up gobs of froth. Gulls coasted on the breeze and complained. Button waved cheerily at an artisan, who ignored him. A girl, hair dourly scarfed, handbag primly clasped, scuttered on, also ignoring his upraised hand. He leant against the metal railings, scanning the shifting water, and felt alone.

She didn't want him.

Sandra Eleanor Margaret Harding. The name could be shortened, and often was.

Looking out over the sea, Button wondered what Sandy was doing now. He could not think that she'd noticed that he'd walked out on her; she'd always ignored his attempts to express his feelings. She misunderstood, misinterpreted, affected deafness. As his father had always said in one of his typical banalities, 'Women are odd fish, and there's an end on't.'

Cautiously Button thought back to their first meeting.

He'd been in the bar of the Grand, oblivious to the gabbling throng, the gin-swilling crowd consulting their programmes. In front of a pillar, apparently looking at him, lounged a girl with blonde hair, abundantly thick over her head. She wore an unusual dress with a frayed hem

54

and patches, stitched, and here and there unstitched, randomly over it. When he smiled she did not shift her stare, still seemed to be taking him in, as he moved towards her.

'Hello,' he said. He was good at that kind of thing.

'Hello.' Her eyes focused on him.

'Enjoying the Chekhov?' he asked. *The Cherry Orchard*.

'Can't understand a word.' An unexpected answer. 'I don't know anyone who says things like they do in this play.'

'Oh, I do.'

'Who are you?' she said. Curious, though not intrigued.

'Edmund Button,' he responded. 'Edmund Braithwaite Williamson Button. I thought you were looking at me when I was standing by the bar.'

'No,' she said. 'I'm short-sighted. I can't see that far.'

Now as he leant against the railings on the promenade he wondered whether he should have understood these early hints. Sandy's behaviour had not altered. Now he saw her as a professional ignorer, inheritor of her father's ability to look through things. Perhaps the message had been there for Button from the start.

She couldn't stand him.

He walked inland along the flat roads, beside the dusty-windowed houses, both dignified and decrepit, scenes Constable wouldn't have touched with a bargepole. He peered through broken-slatted fences into ragged gardens. In one an old woman unpicked seams, then let out a shriek when she saw Button's eye through the fence. An old man passed the time of day over a low wall. 'Nice day. For the time of year. Well, what do you expect?' Button nodded agreement before realizing the old man was talking to someone else.

Looking upwards, he found he could see the sky, huge swathes of blue stippled with cloud. The hills crouched, squashed, trampled, prostrated beneath the opening void of the sky. Men were nothing; cockroaches in their matchbox houses. Here, as a boy, he'd seen the sky; just looked upwards and then, as now, there it had been. Here he'd hoped to bump into the beach-girls he'd drooled over, those tanned, oiled, gleaming leggy girls who filled his dreams. Then, as now, none of them were around. If they had been they'd have ignored him, too. When he wrote his play, it would be about a man, neither young nor old, sitting in a ditch, mumbling half-formed, erratic lines of verse to no one in particular, and being ignored by everyone.

Returning seawards, he assessed his morning. He'd got up; he'd had breakfast; he'd walked down to the promenade; he'd walked inland; now he was walking back to the promenade. Time off. Not answerable to anyone else. It had been a good morning.

'Get lost.'

The words stopped him. A fat man in a raincoat had spoken to another. Both were artisans, neither even mildly interesting.

'What did you say?'

The second man looked uninterested. He picked his nose without hurry.

'You heard.'

'All right then.'

Button watched the exchange. The two men parted, walked away. Was there something interesting happening there? Were the men's words part of an important drama in their lives? Did it matter?

Probably not.

The sun came out watery overhead, curtailing shadows. Button hesitated, not knowing what to do next. He started along the promenade, but five minutes' walking reminded him that he'd already done that once that morning. He found his way into a pub, and ordered a pot of ale.

Here the tables and upholstered settles shone dully in inadequate light. Annoyed, he recognized the man seated with his own jar opposite. John Harding, her father.

Mud-brown eyes in a flesh-coloured face, Harding looked like an electrician who has wired up a plug wrongly and only just remembered to change the wires back again before switching the power on, still a bit shaken, but relieved.

Harding saw him. 'Of all people.'

Button kept his own counsel.

'Beer's not bad.'

Button nodded, placed elbow on arm of settle, said, 'Not bad.'

'Message from my daughter.'

'Oh?' Cautious now, unwilling to overcommit.

'Sandy. Sandra. Sandra Eleanor Margaret Harding.'

'I know.' Button reached in his pocket for spectacles, then remembered he had perfect sight.

The pub was filling with meat-faced men. Their silence showed in the noise.

'Yes, boy,' said Harding.

'Oh?'

Harding drank, complacent, florid, in a second-rate pub, relishing Button's unease. He wiped the spume of ale from his trim moustache, and set his pot down.

'Yes. She says she can't stand you and never wants to see you again.'

'Oh.' Button.

1975

'Hello. Is that Geraldine Byers?'

'Yes, it is,' she replied cautiously into the telephone. The very educated male voice was not familiar to her.

'This is Hawthorne Rackham of the BNA.'

'Ah.' The initials 'BNA' were not familiar to her either.

'I don't believe you are actually a member, are you?'

'A member?'

'Of the BNA.'

'Ah. No. No, I think not.'

'Should be. Naughty girl. We look after your interests.'

'Do you?' She wasn't quite sure of the proper response to this. 'Well, that's very good of you,' she said, playing safe.

'Yes. Well, look, thing is, your name came up in committee yesterday.'

'Did it?'

'Fact is, we were talking about suitable names to join the committee and yours came up.'

'Oh?'

'Feeling was we need some new blood, and people spoke very highly of you.'

'Ah.'

'Said you knew the field very well, whole area of publishing, and that you were, you know, committed to writers' issues.'

'Oh, certainly. I feel one has a duty.'

'One does. One jolly well does. They also said you, you know, hadn't actually got a job apart from the writing and might be able to afford the time.'

Still holding the phone, Geraldine edged her way across her work-room to the bookshelves and reached down the latest copy of *The Writers' & Artists' Yearbook.*

'So,' asked Hawthorne Rackham heartily, 'what do you say?'

'Say?' Geraldine thumbed frantically through to the *Societies and Clubs* section.

'To the idea? Of being on the committee?'

'Well . . .' she replied cautiously, nearly having found her place, 'what would it involve?'

'Basically, the BNA's there to help novelists, a kind of trade body for them.'

'Like the Society of Authors?'

'Well, a bit, but we're rather different.'

'More like the Writers' Guild?'

'Do some similar stuff, but not exactly the same.'

'Like PEN?'

'Again, our interests overlap in a lot of areas, but we do have a very strong separate identity.'

'I see.' Thank God she'd found it. BNA – 'British Novelists Association'. She scanned the entry, as she asked, 'What sort of things do you do specifically?'

'Well, as I say, look after novelists, see that publishers toe the line in their dealings with novelists, raise the profile of novelists . . .'

'Raise the profile?' Geraldine echoed with slight distaste.

Hawthorne Rackham hastened to correct any misleading impression he might have created. 'I mean, discreetly of course. We aren't into any of this dreadful American personality cult nonsense. No, we just want the novelist to be given the respect that is his – or her,' he added punctiliously, 'due.'

'I see.'

'We also administer the Humphrey Halliwell Prize.'

'I don't believe I've heard of it.'

'No, it doesn't get as much publicity as we would wish. One of our problems, really. It was named after Humphrey Halliwell, the lexicographer.'

'And is it for lexicography?'

'No, no, for a novel. Best English novel of the year.'

'A bit like the Booker Prize?'

'Yes, except the Halliwell means just English. None of this Commonwealth nonsense. I mean, the Booker Prize always seems to go to some bloody dago,' he concluded with a hearty laugh.

'I beg your pardon?'

'Oh, nothing, nothing.' He quickly glossed over his fascism. 'As I say, the Halliwell is for a novel. Only two hundred and fifty quid, but better than a slap in the face with a wet fish for some PBA, wouldn't you say?'

'PBA? Do you know, I don't think I'm a member of that either.'

'No, no. Poor Bloody Author.'

'Ah. Yes.'

'Well, what do you feel about joining the committee then?'

'Um . . .'

'We're very keen to get more women on. Make the meetings a bit more decorative, eh?' He laughed fruitily, then seemed to remind himself that attitudes to women had changed in recent years. 'That is, I mean, with this being International Women's Year and all that . . .'

'Yes. You still haven't told me quite how much being on the committee would involve. I mean, I wouldn't want to commit myself to something that's going to take up too much of my time.'

'Of course not.'

'I have just started a new book.' It was true. Ruth Prawer Jhabvala had received the Booker Prize for *Heat and Dust* only a few weeks before. Geraldine wasn't finding it easy to rewrite her *magnum opus* in the new style.

'Yes, of course. Just started a new book – haven't we all, Geraldine, haven't we all? No, thing is, committee meetings are a couple of hours penultimate Tuesday of every month. Start four pip emma, so doesn't take too much of a bite out of the working day.'

'No, that sounds all right. And is that all it involves?'

'Well, there's an annual conference, the odd party – I mean, we are very much a social organization as well as everything else – really doesn't take too long, though.'

'Hm. If I said yes, when would I have to start?'

'Oh, not for a bit. I'm just asking if you'll have your name put up for election, you see. At the AGM, end of January. It all has to be democratic, of course.'

'Oh, so I might not be voted on, anyway?'

'Yes, you will. There are never any nominations apart from the committee ones. Go on, what do you say?'

'Well . . .' Geraldine played the pause for all it was worth. 'Yes. Thank you, Hawthorne, I'm very flattered to be asked and I would like to have my name put up for election.'

After she had put the phone down, she told me later, Geraldine went upstairs and looked at herself in the bedroom mirror. She was wearing a full-length Indian print dress, whose shape seemed to her at that moment to echo the outline of a suffragette. Her face looked, though she said it herself, rather noble. She came to an important decision. It was time that Geraldine Byers became an active defender of writers' rights.

She must become more involved with the great world outside, open out of her writer's isolation, punch picture windows in her ivory tower.

It was for that reason that she had accepted the offer to join the British Novelists' Association committee.

For that reason that she had agreed to tutor a course in Creative Writing.

For that reason that she was accepting an increasing number of engagements to speak at Writers' Circles.

The world of letters had been good to Geraldine Byers. It was time that Geraldine Byers put something of herself back into that world.

Besides, talking about it was a lot easier than actually writing the stuff.

(The above is an example of my reconstruction of Geraldine's telephone conversations from the recordings which she so kindly allowed me to transcribe and – though not really one to blow my own trumpet – I must say I'm rather pleased with the result. I would never dare to compare myself to a real writer like Geraldine, but I am keen to improve on my modest talents, and to vary the approach of my biography, so that it reads as vividly as possible.

Incidentally, I should probably mention that round this time there occurred a change in my own circumstances. I wouldn't mention it if it wasn't relevant to my relationship with the subject of this book.

I had for some time been having difficulty in keeping abreast of the riches of research material that Geraldine so liberally showered on me. I was hard put to keep up to date with indexing all the drafts of her writing, her notebooks, her diaries, and the transcription of her telephone calls was taking up more and more of my time. Imagine therefore how relieved and delighted I was when Geraldine suggested that I should give up my job at the solicitors' and concentrate on the biography full-time!

Though thrilled by the idea, I couldn't help pointing out to my friend that, if I gave up my job, I would have no income. But dear Geraldine had already thought that one through. She would pay me as a housekeeper and, as well as my work on the biography, I might now and then do the odd bit of housework or prepare the occasional meal for her. I would not live in the Holland Park house, but she was sure I would still be able to afford to keep up my flat on the reduced salary.

How typical of Geraldine it was to come up with such an ideal solution to my problems!

I gave in my notice straight away, and gratefully threw myself on to my friend's munificence!)

One of the duties I was more than happy to perform in my new capacity was driving Geraldine to the many Writers' Circles she now addressed. It was a source of undiminishing pleasure for me to see the way she was prepared to share her creative expertise with those less fortunate than herself. One occasion in particular remains in my memory. I still have the image of Geraldine, a magnificently slender figure in knitted wool jacket and thigh-length boots, settling with the minimum of condescension into the very ordinary house of some very ordinary housewife and preparing to give of herself.

'Well, you see, Miss Byers . . .' one of her questioners began.

'Please call me Geraldine.' She gave the altruistic smile of the professional writer taking seriously the problem of the amateur.

'Oh, thank you. Geraldine, I get terrible problems with plotting . . .'

'We all do, we all do.' A ripple of sympathetic laughter ran round the members of the Writers' Circle.

'The thing is,' her interlocutor continued, 'I've got all these ideas in my brain, but I just can't seem to get them down on paper.'

'Well, there you have put your finger on what's been the biggest problem for the writer since he or she had to chip out the words on a stone tablet . . .'

Geraldine Byers was once again under way. I had observed, after driving her to a few of these Writers' Circle meetings, that the same questions came up every time, and could not but admire the speed with which Geraldine had developed her own set answers to them. She spoke with enviable consistency; whatever the question that came up, it would receive one of her perfectly shaped replies, in which, after the first few meetings, she never changed a single word or intonation. How fortunate she was to have been blessed with rhetorical as well as literary skills!

She finished her routine on 'getting ideas down on paper' and was rewarded by a little flutter of applause. Another hand rose with a question. It belonged to a determined-looking woman in her twenties, who had already been ill-mannered enough to question the speaker's advice on how to get a novel started. Knowing her as well as I did, I could recognize the annoyance that tugged at the corner of Geraldine's mouth when she saw the woman's hand.

But there were no other questions. It could not be avoided. 'Yes?' she smiled graciously.

'Do you think it's a writer's duty to reflect what's going on in the world?'

'But of course,' Geraldine replied. 'The writer must be more than a mere entertainer; the writer has a duty as the nation's conscience.'

She had put this so neatly – even aphoristically – that her expression of increased annoyance was quite justified when the young woman pressed on with the supplementary question: 'In what way?'

'Well . . .' said Geraldine, playing for time. 'We have civil wars in Beirut, in Angola . . . we have sectarian violence in Northern Ireland . . . we have over a million unemployed . . . we have piles of bricks in the Tate Gallery . . . we have Dutch Elm disease . . . All these things are grist to the writer's mill.'

'What – so you write about them?'

'I am aware that they are there to be written about,' Geraldine replied judiciously. 'My knowledge of them imparts something to whatever I happen to be writing at the moment.'

'What *are* you writing at the moment?'

'Well . . .'

'I mean, it does seem to me,' the young woman continued pugnaciously, 'that for someone who sets herself up as a writer, you haven't actually had much stuff published.'

Geraldine's nature was too fine to sink to her tormentor's level and counter insult with insult. Instead, she favoured the woman with another charming smile. 'We all work at our own pace, you know. That's one of the most difficult things for a professional writer to find – the appropriate pace of writing.'

'Well, yours seems pretty painfully slow to me,' said the young woman. 'I mean, you haven't published anything for nearly seven years.'

'No, I agree, but — '

'Or have you written lots of stuff, but had it rejected?'

'No!' said Geraldine, whose temper – and who could blame it – was beginning to fray a little at the edges. 'No, I am just concerned about quality. It seems to me that there are too many bad books published, and I don't want to offer my work to the public until I am confident that it is as good as it can be.'

'That sounds to me just like an excuse for — '

'Well, look I'm sure other people have questions to ask. We don't want you hogging our speaker, do we?' The very ordinary housewife who was chairing the meeting, and in whose very ordinary house it was being held, came rather belatedly to Geraldine's rescue. 'Now, any more questions . . . ?'

There weren't any, but rather than run the risk of further ungrateful and ill-informed cavilling, their speaker offered the Writers' Circle a rare treat.

'If you like, I could finish by reading you a little bit from the novel I'm working on at the moment. Work-in-Progress, as it were. Would you like that?'

Duly sensible of the honour, the Writers' Circle murmured enthusiastically that they would like that very much indeed.

'The current title is *Dust and More Dust*, though of course that may change as I go through the "creative process".' Geraldine imparted a thrilling magic to the last two words, the mystery which separated her, the real writer, from her audience, the aspirants.

Then, in her cultured, even voice – that voice I remembered so well from Elocution lessons at school – she began to read.

DUST AND MORE DUST
by
Geraldine Prawer Byers

I don't remember my great-aunts at all, but I have seen their letters. Their letters are old and dusty. It is those letters which brought me first to India.

Fortunately, I kept a journal during the months following my arrival here. It is so easy to forget details, India changes one's perceptions so much, and there is so much dust, that I am glad to have this daily record of what actually happened.

14 April Today Karim Dal invited me to Murapur to see the Nawab's Palace. The heat in the bus was intense and the dust which rose up under the broiling sun filled one's ears and mouth and nostrils. The dusty town of Murapur itself is miserable, little more than a dusty suburb of the Palace itself. Now that great building is empty of people and full of dust, Murapur seems like a town that has lost its purpose (though not its dust).

While we waited in the shade of a dusty tree to be admitted by the watchman, I tried to get Karim Dal to talk about the Nawab, but he was unwilling to say much. He only confirmed the rumours I had heard: that the Nawab had led an evil life of self-indulgence, that there had been scandals. He made no mention of my great-aunts. But, he implied, it was not important. These events were long ago in the past, lost in the dust of time. Inside the Palace, the white, cool rooms and galleries were all empty. Most of the furnishings and decorations had been auctioned, and only the occasional dusty torn brocade curtain or dusty broken throne was left to suggest the splendour which my great-aunts must have witnessed.

1923

The Nawab said 'The house which does not have guests is a dusty house in which no heart beats.' Augusta and Grizelda suspected that this might sound better in Urdu, but were still flattered by his attention, as they had been flattered by his invitation.

He had sent one of the Rolls-Royces to collect them. As they drove towards the Palace at Murapur behind the silent chauffeur, they had relaxed against the pearl-grey upholstery and watched the dust rise from the parched land broiling in the sun. When the angle of the dusty light shifted, they had pulled down the blinds on their windows. The heat was intense and the dust was everywhere. But, in spite of that, they were determined to have a grand time that night.

The Nawab's Palace had been built in the early nineteenth century and was very splendid. As they came out of the dusty heat into its cool elegance, Augusta and Grizelda's eyes lit up at the gleaming rooms with their crystal chandeliers, the tables laid with Sèvres china, the array of silver, the flowers, the crystallized fruits, the absence of dust.

The Nawab's smile of welcome made each of them feel that she at that moment was the only person in the world that mattered. Even if he was just throwing the dust in their eyes, they didn't mind. In the cool of the Palace they could forget the intense heat and dust of the real India outside. In spite of the impoverished dusty villages they had driven through, the lavish decoration of the Palace left them in no doubt about the opulence of their host. How glad they both felt that the third invitation which had arrived for their stepsister had been discreetly dropped into the dustbin. The Nawab continued to smile graciously at them.

'I saw him first,' Grizelda murmured to Augusta through her fixed smile, 'and if you don't let me have first crack at him, there'll be one hell of a dust-up!'

1976

(Selflessly ready, as ever, to do anything that would help me in my biographical task, Geraldine took to carrying a hidden cassette recorder around with her and switching it on when she attended important meetings. What an invaluable archive the transcription of those tapes has been for me!)

'Right, any apologies for absence?' Hawthorne Rackham asked.

Frances Hood, Secretary of the British Novelists' Association from its inception in 1938, answered as promptly as she had done at every other monthly committee meeting for nearly forty years. 'Margot Lockyer can't make it – her mother's not well. Stanley Ribble says he's got a work crisis, getting to the end of a book . . .'

Indulgent laughter greeted the incongruity of this idea.

'And of course Reg has just had his by-pass operation.'

'Oh yes. Have we actually . . . ?'

'Flowers have been arranged.'

'Yes, of course they have. Needn't really ask, so long as you're in charge, need I, Frances?'

She simpered at his compliment. Hawthorne Rackham looked round the green-baize-covered table with its blotters, jugs of lemon barley water and glasses. 'So . . . just us. We few, we happy few,' he said, as he had done at every other meeting during the three years of his Chairmanship. 'Now perhaps we should have last month's minutes . . .?'

While Frances Hood read the last month's minutes, Geraldine Byers looked around at the few, the happy few who were present that afternoon in the crepuscular gloom of the Dilettante Club (a venue which, in common with all other locations where writers' organizations meet, was extremely inconvenient for public transport). There was Wanda Grosely, huge in a purple velvet kaftan; J. Marthwaite Bentley, his eyes doubly veiled by bushy eyebrows and the smoke from his tightly clenched pipe; Lilian Grimshaw, ferociously intelligent behind thick glasses; and Elfrida Elton, propped up in her chair like a patrician stick-insect. All were presumably novelists, since that was the qualification for entry to the BNA, but they all had in common the fact that they hadn't published anything for a very long time.

Frances Hood completed her reading of the minutes. 'Any objections if I put my mark on these?' Hawthorne Rackham demanded heartily.

J. Marthwaite Bentley removed his pipe from his mouth. 'Tiny point, Mr Chairman, but it's recorded that I based my objection to the principle of Public Lending Right on the fact that it would "make the rich richer". In fact, as I recall, my precise words were "it would tend to bring even greater rewards to authors who were already financially established".'

'Oh dear,' said Frances Hood. She was of a nervous disposition and did not enjoy criticism. Most members of the committee, out of deference to this character defect, took care to avoid criticizing her; J. Marthwaite Bentley took pleasure in criticizing her at every opportunity.

Hawthorne Rackham tried to jolly him out of the awkwardness. It was important. Frances Hood had been known to cry at such moments, and that just embarrassed everyone. 'Oh, surely that's pretty much what the minutes say, old boy, isn't it?'

'No, I would say that it definitely isn't.'

'We don't want to split hairs, though, do we?'

'Hawthorne, the BNA is an association made up of people whose business is words. Once we start letting imprecision creep into our use of words in committee, we are betraying our very great heritage.'

'Yes, yes, I see what you mean.' Hawthorne Rackham back-pedalled as cautiously as he could. 'I wonder, Frances love, could we just make the alteration . . . substitute the words J. Marthwaite actually said . . . ?'

'Very well,' said the Secretary, through a little slot of a mouth. There was an uneasy silence. She wasn't going to cry, was she?

But this time, thank God, she didn't. Hawthorne Rackham breathed a sigh of relief for all of them. 'Right, so, with that small change, I'll sign these, and we move on to . . . Secretary's Report.'

While Frances Hood went through the small selection of letters which had trickled through to the BNA postal address, Geraldine Byers confessed to me later that she found her attention wandering. After some eight months on the committee, she was beginning to find that its work was rather predictable. The same subjects circled round, the same precedents were quoted, the same decisions taken and rescinded with monotonous regularity. She didn't want to leave the committee, being on such bodies was important for a literary figure like her, but there were whole quarters of an hour when she knew she could just switch off mentally because she had heard it all before and the same conclusion would be reached as was on the previous occasion a particular subject had come up.

And that day she was full of her new novel. She had had one of those mornings rarely accorded to writers, but which make all the agonies and heartaches of the other mornings worthwhile. The words had flowed, the ideas had flowed, her green Venus 2B pencil had been just another part of that magic conduit between brain and page, directing the crystal streams of pure creativity.

David Storey had won the Booker Prize, and now Geraldine was deeply embedded in her own multi-generational saga of Northern life. It was going wonderfully well. She thought she and George would probably have to have another weekend in York to brush up a few details, but basically she knew the book was marvellous. That was why the time spent in committee was dragging; she longed to be back at the front, going over the top as only a true novelist, high on inspiration, can.

'Now of course there has been a setback recently on the Public Lending Right prospects . . .' Hawthorne Rackham was saying.

'Oh yes, Mr Chairman,' Wanda Grosely agreed. 'That filibuster in the Commons on 17 November has killed it stone dead. It's never going to happen.'

'To my mind,' J. Marthwaite Bentley opined, 'that may not be such a bad thing. As you know, I've always been against the whole idea of Public Lending Right.'

'Yes, I think you have made that point clear. A few times,' said the Chairman. 'But the reason I put the item on the Agenda is because I've had a letter from the Society of Authors once again asking whether we'll join with them in their campaign, or if we're going to keep working on our own separate campaign.'

'Oh, I think we must continue on our own,' Lilian Grimshaw asserted. 'I mean, the Society of Authors deals with all kinds of other writers apart from novelists . . . biographers, translators, all kinds. If we go in with them, we'll lose our identity. I think we in the BNA have a duty to keep out of alliances with other organizations.'

Elfrida Elton endorsed this view, and, as ever, produced a precedent to support it. 'Back in '49 we had an approach from the Society of Authors, asking us to cooperate with them and Garstang, the then Chairman – whom some of you will remember . . .' J. Marthwaite Bentley nodded fondly '. . . refused categorically. He said – and I remember his exact words – "Novelists are, *ipso facto*, individualists, and for individualists to submerge their identity is a contradiction in terms. Co-operation with other organizations is the quick route to nonentity – it is the style of Vidkun Quisling in Norway – and it is something that we should . . . vigorously . . . resist!"'

She could not keep the Churchillian intonation out of the final words, and most of the committee members nodded their concurrence with the former Chairman's views.

Geraldine's mind wandered again. She envisaged a whole new scene of fumbling adolescent love to fit into her Northern saga. She wished she dared to get out a notebook and scribble down a few sentences.

When she was next aware of her surroundings, Hawthorne Rackham was saying, '. . . and we're back to the vexed question of the Awards procedure for the dear old Humphrey Halliwell Prize. Now I think it's very important for the image of the Association that the prize doesn't become regarded as a sort of in-house award, a sort of pat on the back to some loyal BNA committee member from the other BNA committee members . . .'

(He could make this stricture with confidence. He now had nothing to lose, because his last novel had been awarded the Humphrey Halliwell Prize back in the days when still it had been a pat on the back to some loyal BNA committee member from the other BNA committee members.)

'That sort of thing doesn't help the Association's public image at all.'

'But surely, Mr Chairman,' said Geraldine, feeling that perhaps she should get her name in the minutes by saying something, '. . . there's no danger of that happening, because . . .' She was about to say 'because it's so long since anyone on the committee published anything', but, deciding that those present might not wish to have this fact rubbed in, concluded lamely, 'because the public sees it as an objectively-assessed reward for excellence.'

'I'm not sure,' said Lilian Grimshaw bitterly, 'that the public sees it at all. When I won it for *Trugs in the Orchard*, do you know – I didn't get a single mention in a single newspaper in the entire country?'

They did know. It was something she brought up at every committee meeting.

'Well, the only way we're going to get publicity . . .' Hawthorne Rackham's tone of voice showed that he, too, was raising a familiar topic '. . . is by inviting the Press to the Awards Ceremony.'

'What, and *paying* for their dinners?' asked a scandalized Frances Hood, whose duties as Secretary also encompassed those of Treasurer.

'Well, we're back to the old problem,' Hawthorne Rackham sighed, 'of whether we want the BNA to be a private association for its members – the best-kept secret in literature – or whether we want it to raise the public profile of "the novelist" in the Britain of the seventies – and indeed the eighties.'

'I don't think any of us,' Elfrida Elton began magisterially, 'need to be told how *vulgar* is the very notion of publicity in the world of letters.'

'I'm not so sure that I agree with you there,' Lilian Grimshaw protested.

'Well, you have a point,' said J. Marthwaite Bentley, 'but what you forget is that every coin has two sides and on the reverse side of the coin of publicity . . .'

Geraldine Byers sank back into the reverie of her novel. She was on target now, she knew. She was working on the book that really would win her the Booker Prize. And quite possibly the Humphrey Halliwell Prize, too. And any other literary awards that happened to be around at the time. It was really going to be *good*.

SINDALL
by
Geraldine Byers

In the early part of the third decade of the present century a brewer's dray, hauled by a little, coaldust-black pony, made its way through the back-alleys of Gritton, a small south Yorkshire mining village. Beside the driver sat a young woman with a resigned expression and dull blue eyes. She had wrapped over her an old torn blanket, beneath which could be seen the hem of a ragged dress and scuffed broken-down shoes. She gazed blankly about her, as the dray drew up in front of a small, stone-built house, roofed with heavy, misshapen slabs of slate.

'Happen thy s'll have to get off down now, Miss Sindall,' the driver said finally, holding out an arm to help her down. 'I mu'n be on my way. And this be where thy lives, tha knows.'

'Aye,' said the young woman, as she lowered herself down to the dusty cobbles.

'By go, thy's a glum 'un,' the driver said, tightening the rein to the pony, which seemed finally to have lost interest in further travelling. 'Sithee, happen tha sisters s'll have a better time than thy up yonder in York.'

'Aye,' the young woman said. 'Happen. I mu'n get kitchen in shape.'

She watched the dray go: finally, at the turn of the street, the driver turned back, waved cheerily as if there was some reason to feel cheerful about something and vanished, still waving, round the corner of a stone-built terrace.

The young woman went into the kitchen. Through the grimy window she could see the twin headgears of the colliery, the mountains and valleys of slag, grey heaps of ash and clinker that reached out into the fields, finally trickling to nothing at the edge of a coppice. With no fire lit in the hearth, pots still unwashed on the table, she gazed round at the room: there was no comfort there, simply the table, chairs, cupboard, range, sink, pots, pans, plates, dishes, floor, ceiling and walls, which all needed cleaning. She picked up her broom finally and wept.

She had a routine for her work in the house: on Mondays she did the ironing and scrubbed the floors, some of which were covered with linoleum and some not, on Tuesdays did the washing, pummelling the soiled garments against a washboard in the sink. On Wednesdays she tidied her father and sisters' rooms, mounding their dirty clothes into piles and wondering why she hadn't done that on the Monday, because now all their washing would have to wait till the next Tuesday. On Thursdays, she scrubbed and polished the black-enamelled kitchen range till it glowed in the gaslight. On Fridays, she swept through the house, scattering dust over her scrubbed floors and newly-polished range. On Saturdays she remembered she hadn't done any baking and, after burning some small square-shaped loaves, the dough of which refused to rise in a round earthenware bowl in front of the unlit fire, went out to buy some bread, before realizing the shops were closed on a Saturday afternoon. On Sundays she washed the walls, and lit the fire in the black-enamelled fireplace, whose chimney needed sweeping and belched out gritty smoke on to the clean walls. On Mondays she did the ironing and scrubbed the floors, some of which were covered with linoleum and some were not. She worked very hard at her care of the house, but she was absolutely hopeless at it.

1977

Her only thought, Geraldine told me afterwards, as the taxi whisked her along Oxford Street and she saw the punks loitering on the pavements, was how ugly it all was. So ugly . . . and so cold, apart from anything else. The Regent Street lights were up, but had not yet been lit. It really wasn't the weather for half-shaved heads, ripped T-shirts and holey tights. And all that make-up, ugh . . . What lack of confidence it showed in their appearance. At least, Geraldine comforted herself, she had never used cosmetics to hide what she looked like, only to enhance her natural endowments.

No, she liked to think that our generation had had more self-respect when they were that age, more appreciation of how beautiful life was. She couldn't help reacting against the drab hopelessness of young people these days. They really ought to snap out of it.

She realized, she told me later with a slight giggle, that if she had ever vocalized such thoughts she would have sounded terribly crusty. Always the same when she'd spent a weekend down in Gloucestershire with the (increasingly) Aged Parents. But as she grew older, she found she could sympathize a bit more with some of the things they said and thought. Still miles apart politically, of course – better just to keep off subjects like Steve Biko's death, or the Grunwick strike, or trades unions generally while she was down there, anything for a quiet life – but they did talk good sense on a lot of subjects.

Her father's financial situation seemed to have stabilized. He'd finally sold the family's London flat to Arabs at a healthy profit, and that had helped. He wasn't as flush as he'd been in the early seventies, but things seemed to be on an even keel. Certainly, Geraldine had observed no diminution in the customary pampering she had received at the weekend.

She felt good. George was away on business, doing something dreary and chemical in Brazil of all places, and she always felt a slight sense of liberation when she had the house to herself . . . well, virtually to herself – I was there a lot of the time of course, but she didn't really count me. (She and George were still in Holland Park, by the way. One of her New Year resolutions, she told me, was going to be to put the pressure on George and make 1978 the year they finally did move to Hampstead.)

Work was going well. She had started doing a little gentle reviewing which, together with her involvement in the BNA, conveniently filled the gaps between bouts of work on her Booker Book. She had discovered the benefits of pacing her writing, not expecting too much of herself, varying those painful hours of hacking away at the coal-face of her imagination with interludes of gentler intellectual exercise.

Not that the book itself wasn't going well. No, everything very good on that front. Before the announcement of that year's prize, she had confided in me her hopes that Barbara Pym's *Quartet in Autumn* would win – Geraldine quite fancied having a go at the afternoon-tea school of English literature – but, on rereading Paul Scott's *Staying On*, she had become increasingly keen on it. Her own writing took on his style very naturally, and even that morning she had done a useful couple of pages.

But the main reason for her sense of well-being, as Geraldine had told me with a becoming blush when she left the house, was the fact that she was on her way to an assignation. (I was suitably honoured that she trusted me as a confidante for her extramarital as well as her marital confessions. Still, I suppose it's all grist to the biographical mill! I was certainly grateful for the detail in which she recreated the events of her day when she came back that evening, and I felt rather sorry for biographers whose subjects are less forthcoming about their private lives!)

Geraldine had told me often enough about her God-given potential as a *femme fatale*, but it was something she had allowed to lie relatively dormant since marrying George. Now, though, she had decided that it was time to unleash the full power of her sexuality. She was wearing a Jean Muir dress for the lunch (the chemical industry was buying an increasing number of designer dresses these days), and had selected her underwear (Janet Reger, of course) with care.

It was comforting to know, she mused as the taxi edged through Fitzrovia and drew up outside the White Tower, that once a passion had been ignited by Geraldine Byers, its flame would burn forever.

His hair was shorter. What there was of it, which wasn't much. Hardly any on top, and the eaves over his ears were grey now. He wore a pin-striped suit with wide lapels, and a matching striped shirt and tie. But the eyes behind his silver-rimmed glasses sparkled with the same old energy. So Geraldine didn't feel she was lying when she said, 'You haven't changed, Mo.'

He looked puzzled for a moment. 'Oh, sorry. See what you mean.

72

It's just such a long time since I was called that. Most people call me Maurice these days.'

'You'll always be Mo to me.'

'Ah.'

She looked at the dish of olives and radishes, and decided on an olive to nibble. Didn't want too strong a taste on her breath that afternoon. Be hard to avoid garlic, though, in a place as Greek as this. Still, Mo would be having garlic, too.

'How've you been?' she asked.

'Oh, pretty frenetically busy. Autumn's always bad. Frankfurt of course, and then I've been back and forth to the States a few times. Did this Freddie Laker Skytrain, very economical.'

'Oh?'

'And you?'

'Fine, fine.'

'George?'

Geraldine smiled. 'Well, you know George. He doesn't change, does he?'

'No, you're right there.'

It seemed slightly odd that Mo should say this about someone he hadn't seen for nearly ten years, but Geraldine didn't pick him up on it. Instead, she said, 'No, I'm afraid dear old George is never really going to make the hoped-for *rapprochement* with the arts.'

'Ah.'

The conversation was becalmed. Strange, they used always to have so much to talk about. Shyness probably, Geraldine concluded. Be quickly dissipated once they started working down the retsina bottles.

'Care for a glass of wine?' asked Mo, as if hearing her thought.

'Yes, thank you.'

'I stick to mineral water when I'm working. Keep a clear head.'

'Oh.'

'Still don't let me inhibit you if you fancy a drop.'

'Well, just a glass might be nice.'

'So you haven't got anything planned for this afternoon?'

She looked at him sharply. Had there been a sexual overtone in his question? If there had, she concluded with slight disappointment, it had been well-disguised. 'No, no, nothing special,' she replied.

'Now let me think, you always used to do your writing in the mornings, didn't you?'

'Yes.' She relaxed a little. This vein of mutual reminiscence could prove to be a rich one.

'Between eight and ten, wasn't it?'

'Seven and nine.'

'Oh yes. That's when you were working for that crummy magazine . . . what was it called . . . ? *Fulcrum* . . . ?'

'*Pivot.*'

'Right, right.' A longish pause. 'So have you been pounding the keyboard again this morning?'

'I still write the same way I always did, Mo. Green Venus 2B pencil in orange-covered feint-ruled school exercise books.'

'Oh.' He sounded as if he was hearing this information for the first time.

'I don't type.'

'I didn't mean typing. I assumed you had graduated to one of these new word processors. I'm sure George can afford it.'

Geraldine recoiled. 'Good heavens, no!' The idea of technology coming between her and the pure flow of her imagination was as unappealing as the idea of inhibiting her creativity by excessively detailed research.

'You'll come round to it.'

A little knowing shake of the head. 'I don't think so, Mo.'

'You will. Have you tried one?'

'No.' She was as affronted as a nun being asked if she had snorted cocaine.

'You should. They'll come down a lot in price. Soon every writer in the country'll be using one.'

'Every writer except me,' she corrected him tartly.

The breeze impelling their duologue once again dropped. Geraldine took a long swallow from her glass of retsina and struggled to overcome the conversational inertia. 'What have you been up to in the States, Mo?'

'Oh, trying to sort out some deals with the film companies. You know, spin-off stuff. If you can get hold of the English end of something like a *Star Wars* book, or *Saturday Night Fever*, well, you're going to clean up.' He grimaced. 'Mind you, the Americans have got all that very tightly sewn up.'

'Hmm. Yes, I suppose that kind of book can subsidize the rest of your list.'

'What?'

'Well, the literary fiction, that kind of stuff.'

'Ah.' After a silence, he began diffidently, 'Actually, Geraldine, there was a reason why I suggested we met for lunch . . .'

She half-closed her eyes and gave him a little smile. This was more like it. She had been over in her mind how she should play the scene when he finally got round to the subject on both their minds. She did not want to appear too avid, not as if she were making herself cheap, but she wanted to leave him in no doubt of the continuing latent heat of her smouldering sexuality.

'Thing is, Geraldine, I was wondering whether we could do a book together . . .'

It was certainly a different approach. But she did not find it wholly unappealing. She had visions of sitting close over sheets of manuscript, drawing closer, then abandoning their green Venus 2B pencils in a sudden blur of paper-fluttering passion.

'Oh yes?' she murmured in her darkest chocolate voice.

'Thing is, I mean, I know you can write . . .'

She graciously acknowledged the truism.

'And you know a bit about history . . .'

'Well . . .'

'Enough to do this kind of thing, anyway . . .'

'Mm?'

'And I'd have thought you'd got enough experience . . .'

'Oh yes,' Geraldine agreed with an intimate smile.

Mo put his hands, as if they were his cards, on the table. 'What I'm talking about, Geraldine, is a "bodice-ripper".'

'A bodice-ripper,' she echoed chillingly.

'Yes, you know, bit of sex, bit of violence, vague historical background . . . They're going over big at the moment. I've got a deal sorted out on this between P & L and an American publisher, getting a list together, could do very well.'

Geraldine put on her haughtiest Virginia Woolf look. 'And what makes you think I could write that sort of book?'

He misunderstood her objection. 'I'm sure you could, love. Just a matter of believing in yourself. It's all writing, after all, and you can write, can't you?'

'I meant,' she said severely, 'what made you think I would want to write that kind of book?'

'I thought you'd appreciate the offer. Thought I'd be giving you a nice break, chance to make a few bob. Look, if you can come to the office in Long Acre one of these days, I've got a new editor who could — '

'Maurice,' she announced with magnificent righteousness, 'I am not the sort of writer who writes to make a few bob.' It was remarkable that the last few words didn't shrivel up and die in the venom with which she steeped them.

'Oh, you mean you're busy? What are you working on at the moment?'

'I have recently started a new work of literary fiction,' she replied icily. 'A book rather in the manner of Paul Scott.'

'Sorry?'

75

'Author of *Staying On*. Recent winner of the Booker Prize.'

'Oh.'

'Also of *The Raj Quartet*. You know, *The Jewel in the Crown*, that lot. Set in India.'

'Doesn't sound very commercial to me.'

'Of course it's not commercial!'

'You want to keep away from that kind of stuff. Go for the sort of books that are going to have spin-offs. You know, television series, that kind of thing.'

Geraldine's response found as yet uncharted levels of *hauteur*. 'I cannot imagine the day when a work like *The Raj Quartet* will feature as a television series.'

'No.' Mo looked pensive. 'So I'm to take it you aren't interested in my offer?'

'That is exactly how you are to take it.'

'Well, I don't know what else I can suggest, really . . .'

'You don't have to suggest anything.'

'No, but I mean, like, now P & L's really swinging along, I'd like to do you a favour, like, for old time's sake.' Neither the lapse into his former style of speech nor the mention of 'old time's sake' had a thawing effect on Geraldine's frozen expression of affront, but he did not seem aware of it. 'I don't know, unless we go into a different area completely. I mean, books like that Bay City Rollers one did pretty big sales. You don't know anything about the Sex Pistols by any chance, do you, Geraldine . . . ?'

When she got back to Holland Park, she came straight to where I sat transcribing her phonecalls. She was still smarting from the appalling insults she had suffered and, in the white-heat of her anger, relayed to me every word that had been spoken at lunch.

An hour later, when she had finished, she changed out of the Jean Muir dress, out of her carefully-chosen Janet Reger underwear, and put on her writing clothes.

To calm herself down and reassure herself of her true artistic destiny, she then read through the latest chapter of her Booker Book.

STAYING PUT
by
Geraldine Byers
Chapter Nine

Bhutan liked working for Jumbo Hardacre because a sahib like that could almost make him forget the ending of the *raj*. Jumbo Sahib had a proper attitude to the treatment of servants, almost as members of the family, who could be bawled out or complimented according to his mood, but who were still really in charge of the situation and who could subtly help themselves to the many little perks which their employers' households offered. Bhutan detested taking orders from jumped-up Indian nobodys, but was never happier than when being sworn at by a Sahib like Jumbo.

A bellow sounded from the verandah. Bhutan carefully drained the rest of the gin, braving the displeasure of the Prophet, wiped the glass clean with a cloth, replaced it on the sideboard and went to answer his master's summons.

'Sahib wants?' he inquired, going out to the verandah, where Jumbo lounged in a cracked cane chair.

'Want my bloody daughter, you silly bugger! Where is she?'

'Memsahib at hairdresser in Ashtaz Hotel.'

'Why is she never bloody here when I need her?'

'She always here, Sahib. Only not here when she go to hairdresser or she go alone to movies.'

'Don't argue with me, you bloody scoundrel! I say she's never here when I want her!'

'Sahib knows best,' Bhutan conceded with a little bow, which stayed just the right side of insolence.

'Watch it, Bhutan. You try it on with me and you'll be out on your ear! Got that?'

'Yes, Sahib.'

Bhutan looked pleased. It was some weeks since Jumbo Sahib had threatened to sack him. Not since before Sahib had been sick. So the threat was a sign that he was on the mend. Jumbo Sahib still looked ill, the flesh hanging slackly from his bones, skin pale under its blotches and freckles, but the fact that he was once again swearing with something approaching his customary vehemence was an encouraging sign.

'And is my bloody daughter going to the movies tonight?'

'Oh yes, Sahib. Monday nights she always goes to movies. Tonight Repeat Showing Bonnie and Clyde. Warren Beatty, Faye Dunaway. Very good gangster film. Memsahib ask me to book usual seat. Second House.'

'Leaving me alone tonight again, the silly cow?'

'No, please, Memsahib not wish to leave you alone. Sahib go also to movies? I book two seats?'

'No, you bloody halfwit! I don't need to see films about gangsters. Only have to look at the bitch who owns the lease on this place to see the real thing. Go and get me a bloody *chota peg*! Big one.'

Bhutan shook his head in mild reproach. 'Doctor Amitraj say Sahib only drink beer after — '

'Bugger the doctor! Do as you're bloody told or you'll be out on your arse!'

Bhutan withdrew gracefully. The Sahib's voice followed him. 'And get those sodding canna lilies watered too, while you're at it!'

Bhutan smiled. It was not only the canna lilies that would be watered. He would do his duty for Dr Amitraj and the Memsahib (Bhutan decided) by watering the *chota peg* as well. He smiled for another reason, too. Jumbo Sahib was nearly back to his old cantankerous self. It was as it should be.

Jumbo Hardacre looked out over the grey-green hills, resolutely keeping his eyes off the glass and concrete tower of the Ashtaz Hotel to his left. Only make me bloody angry. Start me thinking about the damn' bitch who owns the place. And my place. Great Scott, just to think of that cow brings up my blood pressure. She thinks the sun shines out of her bloody arse.

Never mind. Don't think about the bitch. She'll make a balls-up somewhere along the line, get her comeuppance. Bloody Punjabis always do. Think about something else. Letter from the girls came in the *dak* this morning. Seem to be having a bloody good time back in the old country. Whale of a social life, getting invited to balls, that kind of caper. Right thing for them to go back. Wrong for me. Too bloody old. Been in India nearly fifty years. Spots a bit too engrained to be rubbed out now.

Right thing for Lucinda to stay out with me, though. Arguments for her going back when the other two went, but wouldn't have worked out. Besides, someone got to run this place. Bloody useless on my own. Cackhanded as an ape with gloves on. Couldn't manage alone since the proper Memsahib kicked the bucket. Need someone to talk to the servants, anyway. Comes better from a woman. Oh, I can bawl the lazy buggers out all right, but when it comes to organizing a dinner party or that kind of shooting-match, about as useless as a spare prick at a wedding. No, makes sense for Lucinda to do all that.

Besides, there's the money. Damn' expensive, life in England, and going up all the time. Just about scraped together enough loot to get the other two back, but had to draw the line somewhere. When I pop off, Lucinda'll get the Life Insurance, which'll be at least £2000, maybe a bit more with profits. That'll take her home if it's what she wants. Though she might do better staying put out here. Find some clot to marry her. Not an Indian of course. Perish the thought. No, but even now chaps come out to advise on government projects, guff like that. All she needs to do is find one who's woozy with a touch of sunstroke, get him to pop the question (Ha!), and Bob's your uncle.

Lucinda sat under the drying-helmet and sneaked a look at her watch. Bhutan would have the tonga waiting for her at 8.30 a.m. In good time. Jane had trimmed, shampooed and rinsed her hair early, as usual, at the cut rate they had agreed. No need for panic.

But she couldn't help a little feeling of panic at the thought of the crackly air-mail letter clasped in her handbag. She always felt trapped when she had a letter from England. It was only slowly that she had realized her father, Jumbo, never intended to go home. At first, when the other two went, she had thought it was only a matter of time. Time for the money to be saved, time for some insurance policy to mature, and then they'd all be back in England.

But that wasn't going to happen. When he died, in a couple of years, maybe sooner, she would be alone. There would be no one of her own race, of her own colour, to comfort her. She would have to take some kind of job, teaching perhaps, to avoid destitution. She would lose all status, even the spurious title of 'Memsahib', so inappropriately imposed on her after her stepmother's death. She would be nobody. She couldn't bear to think of it.

The letter had not been from her sisters. No, of course not. She always heard what they were up to from a third party. This time it had been Sarah Wellsby-Newton (Yuill-Pinkerton that was). A chatty letter, full of little irrelevancies, shopping, theatres, parties, things that Sarah could take for granted and that she, Lucinda, could only dream of.

But the part of it that hurt was the casual reference to one particular social event. 'You probably don't recall a very pleasant young man called Sharwood (like the curries). You might have met him when he was out in Pankot four or five years back.'

Oh yes, she had met him. He had been her first sexual object. She had been far too young for him to notice at the time, but she remembered precisely the line of his jaw and the tight seams of the light beige suit that he wore. Then he, like everyone else, had gone back home, unaware of the adolescent passion he had woken in her.

Since then, she saw him time and again, in the turn of a tourist's shoulder, in a film-star's profile at the movies, in the smile of a model in a magazine advertisement at the hairdresser. Sharwood. Sharwood. Are you happy? Do you ever think of me? Do you remember me at all? What do you think of me? If anything?

But yes, he did remember her. It was in Sarah's letter, something so precious to Lucinda, so casually thrown away in correspondence. She remembered Sarah's precise words, though the letter was still locked in her handbag. 'Anyway, Sharwood's suddenly turned up on the London scene, and invited everyone to some massive "do" he's laying on. Don't know what it's in aid of, but all sounds pretty lavish. Apparently he's not married or anything, so I've no idea what he's up to. I've had an invite. So've your sisters and – this is the funny thing – he also sent one for you. Obviously thought the whole family'd come home, didn't realize you were staying put in Pankot with Jumbo. Thought you might be interested to hear about the "shindig", thought obviously you won't be able to put in an appearance. Still, it's the thought that counts, after all, isn't it?'

Jane came to lift up the drier, with her hands that were so dark, so definitely *of the country*. Deftly she removed the rollers, combed the hair out and raised a mirror for her client's inspection. 'There, that looks perfect, doesn't it, Miss Hardacre? Only English women have such fine hair and skins. Next time perhaps we will try a beehive?'

'Yes, maybe,' Lucinda murmured, then paid her bill, tipped Jane cautiously, and went out to the waiting tonga.

1978

Geraldine Byers still saw Virginia Rawson from time to time, and it was to Virginia that she turned when she finally decided that she needed an agent.

As I had painfully witnessed, the year had been one of frustrations for Geraldine. Having finally persuaded George that a move to Hampstead was essential to her development as an artist and to the health of their marriage, she had then got caught up in a tedious cycle of buyers falling through, chains breaking and purchasers changing their minds (not at all the kind of domestic trivia which should be allowed to distract the attention of a serious novelist from her God-given mission). By December, when the housing market went quiet in the run-up to Christmas, the move was still not sorted out. Geraldine blamed George. It was a habit she had dropped into.

Nor was her creative life any more fulfilling. She was beginning to get a bit bored with the BNA, with the dreary circuit of Writers' Circles, and the Booker Book was not going well. She had felt really at home with *Staying Put* and got nearer to completing it than any of her previous efforts. But then what had been intended to be a 'working holiday' in a farmhouse in the Dordogne with George and a married couple of writers and another unmarried couple of writers and Virginia (and me generously included to do the cooking!) had ended up being simply an 'eating, drinking and sleeping holiday', so that the book had slipped behind in the time-scale she had mentally allocated for it.

As a result, when Iris Murdoch's Booker Prize victory for *The Sea, the Sea* was announced, Geraldine was faced by a real dilemma for the first time since she had started on her quest. Should she spend a few more weeks completing *Staying Put*, or should she bow under the yoke she had imposed on herself, put its manuscript into the same cupboard as the accumulated orange-covered school exercise books of the last ten years and start her Iris Murdoch novel? Eventually, after much late night agonizing, shared by George when he was there and me when he wasn't, she decided that she must follow her predestined course and start writing *The Spray, the Spray*. But she reached the decision with anguish, and did not

81

leave George unaware of the fact that she blamed him for the situation.

It is always hard for artists to attribute causes to their creative malaise, but Geraldine came up with the list of impediments (apart from their spouses) which all writers turn to when the work's going badly: their geographical location, the physical objects with and on which they write, their publishers and their agents (or lack of agents).

The unsatisfactory nature of her geographical location was something of which Geraldine was all too painfully aware. She felt choked in the philistinism of Holland Park and longed to breathe the pure intellect of Hampstead. But everything that could be done was being done, so she could only wait for that particular improvement in her working conditions to happen.

In the matter of her writing materials, she suffered a cruel blow towards the end of 1978. Having made the painful decision to abandon *Staying Put* – or at least rewrite it in a different style – she went dutifully along to the stationers to replace her dwindling stock of orange-covered school exercise books.

This was part of her fascinating ritual as a writer. Just as they always had to be identical exercise books, so they had always to be purchased from the same stationers, where she had bought the original orange-covered exercise book in which she had inscribed the first, potent sentence of *Pale Cast of Thought*. The shop was in Bloomsbury, because she had been working at *Pivot* when she began her first novel.

Imagine her shock, therefore, when she arrived at the stationers in the November of 1978 to find that they did not have any of the all-important orange-covered exercise books in stock. Worse news was to follow, however. Not only were they not in stock, they would never be in stock again! The company which manufactured them had gone into liquidation! The stationer offered a selection of feint-ruled exercise books in colours that ranged through the spectrum, but could not provide the precise objects which were so much part of the arcanum of Geraldine Byers' craft.

This setback threw her into depression for a week, while she tried to decide what colour she should home in on. At times she even contemplated the heresy of giving up writing altogether, then the lesser blasphemy of following Mo's advice and just writing something people might want to read. This was truly the dark night of her soul as a novelist, and it was only by a huge effort of will and plentiful reminders to herself of her exceptional talent that she was able to overcome her doubts. (I like to think that I may have made my own modest contribution to her recovery. I certainly spent most of that week listening to her agonizing and, though of course I couldn't know the true depths of her pain, perhaps just my being there late into the nights helped a bit.)

Eventually, reluctantly, but driven by her sense of destiny, Geraldine purchased a supply of pink-covered feint-ruled exercise books. Valiantly she wrote on in them. But it wasn't the same. She blamed George and dreaded the moment when the Venus pencil company would go out of business.

The next object of justified blame was her publisher. Geraldine reflected bitterly on how much Abrams & Willis undervalued her work, how much they took for granted her remarkable talent and the honour of having her name on their list, how pitifully few of her books they had printed, and how little they had budgeted for the promotion of Geraldine Byers. In a fit of righteous indignation, she made up her mind to change publishers forthwith. She even rang Sidney Parrott to tell him her awesome decision.

Insensitive man that he was, he seemed remarkably underwhelmed by the news. He said that the only sanction in the relationship between them was an option clause at the end of her contract for *Pale Cast of Thought*, by which she, on her side, undertook to show any new work 'of a similar nature' to Abrams & Willis first, and they, on their side, undertook to make an offer for the book within six weeks if they wanted it. But, Sidney continued, option clauses were being constantly broken these days and he could guarantee that Abrams & Willis would take no legal action if she wished to offer her next novel elsewhere. Anyway, it was all a bit academic, wasn't it, until she actually had a completed manuscript. And he was sorry, but he had to dash, seeing an American publisher. He didn't even invite her out for lunch.

Geraldine was extremely aggrieved – and who could blame her? This was just another distressing incident, she pointed out to me, in the continuing history of abuse of authors by publishers. Milton had only been paid five pounds down for *Paradise Lost*, with another five pounds promised after the first thirteen thousand copies had been sold; and since then the circumstances of writers hadn't noticably improved.

She was, quite reasonably, furious. She had to do something, but she couldn't be expected to do it on her own. She contemplated taking her case to the British Novelists' Association, but a brief reflection on the efficiency of that body dissuaded her. There was another course open to her, though. One thing *had* changed since Milton was writing; now there were literary agents around to pick up cudgels on the author's behalf. Since the start of her literary career, Geraldine had handled all negotiations herself, seduced, she could see in retrospect, by Sidney Parrott's meaningless flannel about authors' loyalty and marriages between authors and publishers. But now the moment had come for change. Geraldine Byers was going to get an agent, an ally in her battle against the iniquities of publishers.

She rang Virginia Rawson for advice on suitable names. '. . . I mean obviously not yours, Virginia, but I thought you might know the scene.'

'Why not mine?'

'Well, um . . .' It was slightly difficult to make her point tactfully. 'I'm sure yours is frightfully good on, you know, your sort of thing, crime, what-have-you, category stuff . . . but, as you know, what I write is more in the nature of literary fiction.'

'My agent deals with literary fiction, too.' It almost sounded as if there was a laugh in Virginia's voice as she said this. Must have been a fault on the line.

'Oh, and what's his name?'

'*Her* name. Sheila Diamond. Very good, very tough.'

'Sounds ideal. I need someone tough. Could you give me an introduction to her, please?'

'I'll ring her if you like. She claims always to be on the look-out for good new authors, but . . . her standards are pretty high.'

'I feel confident that I can meet them,' said Geraldine glacially.

Virginia rang back within ten minutes. 'Well, I've mentioned your name.'

'Oh, thank you. So shall I expect a call from her?'

'Um, no. I think you'll probably have to ring her.'

Geraldine tried ringing straight away, only to be told by the girl on the switchboard that Sheila Diamond was in a meeting. Geraldine got me to keep ringing again at half-hourly intervals, but the meeting apparently went on for the rest of the day. And the next day.

Geraldine curbed her anger. After all, she reasoned it out to me, the agent must be unavailable because she was busy fighting battles for her clients, being tough. When Geraldine was on the agency's books, it would be her battles that Sheila Diamond was fighting, on her behalf that the toughness would be manifested.

I eventually got through on the morning of the third day, and handed the telephone over to Geraldine. 'Yes, what do you want?' asked an aggressive voice from the other end.

'Sheila Diamond?'

'Yes,' the voice confirmed testily.

'I'm ringing at the suggestion of Virginia Rawson . . .'

The name slightly softened the agent's tone. 'And . . . ?'

'My name is Geraldine Byers. I believe Virginia mentioned me.'

'She may have done. What is it?'

'I am, needless to say, a writer, and I think I'm in need of an agent.'

'Oh? What have you written?'

'I had a novel called *Pale Cast of Thought* published by Abrams & Willis.'

'Haven't heard of it. When was this?'

'1968.'

'Look, you don't have to give me the full prehistory. What have you published recently?'

'Well, nothing since then.'

'Nothing?'

'No.'

'And have you just finished something now?'

'No. I've just started something, though.'

'Then why the hell are you wasting my time!'

'I beg your pardon?'

'Listen, Miss . . . What-ever-your-name-was, a literary agent sells a commodity. That commodity is a book. A completed book. If you aren't the possessor of a completed book, then we have nothing to talk about!'

'But when I have completed the book . . . ?' asked Geraldine pitifully.

'When you have completed the book, you can bloody well . . .' But the agent relented and didn't complete her sentence as she had first intended. Biting her lip, she continued, 'When you have completed the book, I will have a look at it.'

'Oh, thank you.'

'And I only say that because Virginia Rawson is such an important author, that if she asks for a favour I have to listen. Think yourself lucky you know her.'

'An important author? Virginia's only — '

But the phone had been put down the other end before Geraldine could finish what she was going to say.

After the conversation, she angrily listed to me some of the things she should have said. That she was an important literary figure, that she did some reviewing, that she was on the BNA committee, that she spoke frequently to Writers' Circles, that when her first novel had come out it had been hailed by the *Stroud Advertiser*, no less, as 'promising'.

But it was too late to make these points. All we could do was to commiserate with each other about the ignorance of true worth which is so endemic in the modern world of publishing.

Geraldine had the advantage over me that she could channel the energy of her anger into her novel. The one which really was going to win the Booker Prize this time.

God, though, I could understand why she kept saying what hell it was being a writer.

THE SPRAY, THE SPRAY
by
Geraldine Byers

The spray which rises over the rocks before me as I write catches glints and shards of light in the weak October sun. The sky at its highest is dull charcoal. It lightens as it descends through the cloud to a paler metallic grey, then melts to the shifting greyness of the sea. Closer to the shore, the metal is silvered, brighter, not lighter however, but less dull, though still quite dull. Right up against the rocks the silver turns to deep blue, shot through with the white of the spray.

That paragraph of rather fine writing, destined to be the start of my autobiography, was interrupted by an event so bizarre and ghastly that, even though many months have passed, and I may have begun to understand what happened, I still cannot call it to mind without an almost physical revulsion. Perhaps I will feel more able to cope with it tomorrow.

No, I don't.

It is now a week since I last picked up my pen to tackle this autobiography, or diary, or memoir, or whatever it may turn out to be, and the horror that kept me from it has receded a little. Inevitably, as a man of the theatre, I must write of that cradle of illusions, that arena of fantasy, though its rough magic I abjured, not here where I watch the spray, but long ago, when I made my farewell bow in that fated production with Hubert, Caspar, Inigo, Amyas and Theophila.

Three more days have passed. I have been swimming (naked). For breakfast I had a bowl of cornflakes, sprinkled with a little cinnamon, followed by two slices of wholemeal toast covered with Greek honey. I had hoped for guavas too, but these proved beyond the resources of the village shop (which seems to rely chiefly on its post office as an attraction for customers). I feel perhaps now I dare to introduce myself to you, my reader, assuming you exist, or, if not, *faute de mieux*, to myself. Though I have garnered a degree of fame in my life, I will not be so arrogant as to presume that my name is familiar to you (though it is of course to me, if you *don't* exist – well, I mean, I've known it all my life, after all, haven't I?). Very well, I am Roland Caraway and, at the time of writing, have to admit to over sixty. I have never been married and have long since put the theatre behind me (in spite of urgings that I should make a comeback from Spencer, Ottilie, Tristram, Ethelred and Keith).

It is after lunch now. For lunch, you will be interested to know, I had tinned baby scallops, served with diced mushrooms, celeriac, radicchio, endive, sweet potato, fennel and salsify (the village shop has certainly taken my criticisms to heart), with just a touch of vinaigrette. I washed this down with a bottle of (delicious) Sancerre. How important food is. Philosophy and music may massage the soul, but food keeps us alive. Properly lunched and agreeably drunk, I should now perhaps describe the house. But that could take forever and, as I am feeling extremely sleepy, I think I'll have a nap instead.

Reading these paragraphs again, I get a nasty feeling I may be giving a false impression. It's no fun writing this sort of stuff, let me tell you (still, of course, assuming you exist). I worry that, in what I have written, I have not yet said enough about the sea and the spray, nor filled you in on the details of my past emotional life, and I've a feeling that those deficiencies should be remedied as soon as possible.

Perhaps I should start with the letter from Torquil that arrived this morning, stirring anew memories that I thought lay buried at the bottom of the sea, below the spray. I will transcribe what he wrote.

> Roland, what are you up to, you old fraud? Klaus, Lachlan and Hallam all swear you've gone peculiar, and I'm beginning to half-believe it myself. I need to talk to you about the business between Juno and Cynara, and since I can't raise you on the telephone, I'm going to bloody well come down and see you.

As you can imagine, this was not welcome news. The mention of Juno and Cynara made me half-mad. I rushed around the house, banging into furniture, up and down the stairs, into the conservatory. I drank a lot of whisky, took a sleeping pill and tumbled head first into sleep. I dreamt I saw Cynara beside the pumpkin, wearing all her finery, but with no head.

When I was young I never knew whether I was the one who didn't exist or Juno was. It was somehow obvious that the real world wasn't big enough for both of us. Juno always had a touch of the ethereal about her and, though I was unworried when she took up with Marcel after he'd decided he wasn't queer and broken up Mervyn's marriage by going off with Perpetua, I did begin to feel a degree of disquiet over her relationship with Cynara. There was a psychological symbiosis about them, whether together or apart, which seemed to transcend the mere community of interest one might expect between godmother and goddaughter.

Still, I, as Cynara often told me with relish, was a boring old fart, who should stick to his theatrical memories and idiosyncratic cooking and swimming naked, leaving them to get on with life. God, how little the young and arrogant care what they say.

'I believe only in what defies belief,' Juno announced.

I was in her flat in Bloomsbury, that strange junk shop of squatting Buddhas, brass pagodas, devil-masks, lacquer paintings of lotuses, philosophical tracts, chrysanthemums, of the sea and the spray. In brass trays lay jointed rings and necklaces, bejewelled daggers, pumpkins, frail china figurines and prayer-wheels.

Perhaps I should describe Juno to you. On the other hand, perhaps I should let you use your imagination.

'But is belief that important to a believer?' I asked, picking up the point that she had made a good few paragraphs back. 'Surely it's over-simplistic to go off into some cloud of unknowing just when the knowable becomes accessible.'

Juno laughed harshly. '*Cakum habere edereque impossiblile est.*'

'Not with you?'

'You can't have your cake and eat it.'

I was disgusted in the kitchen this morning to see a rat, six mice and six lizards. When I looked again, they had gone. I suppose they were not doing any harm. Such creatures have as much right to exist as anyone else, after all, don't they?

I did a bit of shopping, went for a swim (naked of course), and for lunch cooked snails in a delicate sauce of kale, broccoli, lima beans, okra, pumpkin and boletus edilis: lovely stuff!

I will now describe what happened next, though most of it still seems inexplicable, if not impossible. Certainly any calm which the day had promised up until that moment gave way to a frenetic sequence of horrors whose recollection can still shake me.

We got drunk. That was certainly true. And started singing. Tobias was there, with his mistress Linette, together with Ghislaine, for whom, to my surprise, I found all my desire had faded. Lloyd was also present, of course, with Jesse and Geraint.

'I don't love you, Ghislaine,' I said.

'You're drunk.'

'I may be drunk, but even if I were sober, I still wouldn't love you.'

'Oh, love, love – why all this fuss about love?'

'What else should we make a fuss about?'

'Why not just not make a fuss about anything?'

'It's a thought, Ghislaine. It's certainly a thought.'

What a bizarre facsimile of happiness that evening becomes in retrospect. Everything so innocent, so undisturbingly incomprehensible, until the moment that the dreadful thing happened. From then on, all is confusion, fragmentation, recollections shattered like a wave breaking in spray on the dark rocks below.

Suddenly Cynara was standing in the doorway. She wore a dress that glittered in the candlelight. We stared at her, testing our eyes against drunkenness.

'Juno has arranged everything,' she said. 'I am going to get into my coach now.'

I was shattered. Everything I had believed up to that point crumbled around me. Some sleeping demon had been awakened, some deathly gin-trap sprung; and only the future could hold the answers to the questions that had not yet been asked.

1979

'But surely it's a great achievement for the Women's Movement?'

'I'm honestly not sure,' said Geraldine. I could see from the other side of the room, where I was trapped by a marine insurance broker, that her eyes were beginning to glaze over. But she bravely kept the conversation going. 'Mrs Thatcher doesn't seem to have given much support to her sex so far.'

'No, but it's early days,' the woman said. 'Give her a chance. Ooh, did you see that thing they did about Mrs Thatcher on *Not the Nine O'Clock News* the other night?'

'No. I'm afraid I don't watch much television.'

'Well, you miss a lot.'

'Really?'

'Yes. But going back to Mrs Thatcher . . . I think just the fact that we now have a woman Prime Minister is enormously important. Wouldn't have happened five years ago.'

'Maybe not.' Geraldine was finding, as ever, that her attention strayed when politics were being discussed. I heard her trying to manoeuvre the conversation round to something important. 'Have you read the new Fay Weldon?'

'No,' the woman replied.

'Now I think she's very interesting from the woman's viewpoint.'

'Oh. I haven't heard of her. What was the name again?'

'Fay Weldon. *Praxis* was shortlisted for the Booker Prize.'

'Oh, fancy that. 'Fraid I haven't heard of the Booker Prize either. Still, never mind . . .' The woman giggled. 'And what's your husband's line of country?'

'I beg your pardon?'

'Your husband – what does he do?'

'Oh, he's in chemicals.'

'That could mean anything. What exactly does he do in chemicals?'

'Well, *I* don't know, do I?' Geraldine replied with something approaching testiness. I realized how difficult it must be for her to keep polite talking to a woman as stupid as this one. 'Have you read the new V. S. Naipaul?'

'What?'

'Oh, never mind.'

The woman giggled at some private recollection. 'You'll never guess what my four-year-old did today . . .'

'No, I'm sure I won't,' Geraldine agreed drily.

'Well, the thing is, Nigel, that's my husband – you haven't met him yet, have you, he's with Shell – anyway, he'd been putting up some ceiling tiles, and we'd got this tub of the fixing cement stuff in the bathroom and Josh – that's our four-year-old – well, he went up to the bathroom and . . .'

As the woman launched into her interminable anecdote, I could see Geraldine straightening her *Annie Hall* waistcoat, and looking around the room. I knew exactly the thoughts that would be going through her head. That there must be somebody at the party simply dying to talk about literature to as serious an enthusiast and practitioner as Geraldine Byers. But there didn't seem to be. The only other writer in evidence was good old Virginia Rawson, listening to George with what – unlikely though it might seem – appeared to be interest.

Geraldine was clearly annoyed. Having finally achieved the long-awaited move to Hampstead, she had been invited to too many parties like this one. She had been hoping for a kind of *salon* atmosphere, a sustained flow of informed literary badinage, a free exchange of bookish thoughts among like-minded souls, but all too often she had ended up cornered by some ghastly woman like this one, talking about children and television programmes and husbands' jobs and Mrs Thatcher and ceiling tiles. Ceiling tiles, for God's sake! What had a fine mind like Geraldine Byers' to do with ceiling tiles?

There had been one party she'd been to since they moved, where the hostess claimed that Margaret Drabble had dropped in earlier, and that Melvyn Bragg was expected to drop in later. But he hadn't appeared. Sometimes it seemed to her that the whole world conspired to keep Geraldine Byers out of her proper *milieu*.

She became aware that the ceiling tile woman was asking her a question. 'I'm sorry?'

'I said: Do you have any children?'

'Children? Er, no.'

'Oh. Bad luck.'

Geraldine responded with the opinion that she had often expressed to me. 'I have never felt my lack of children to be bad luck. I am sure they would only distract me from my work.'

'Oh, you're a "career woman", are you? Got your eyes on Number Ten then, like Mrs Thatcher, have you?' The woman giggled.

'No,' Geraldine replied chillingly, before enunciating the primary article of her faith. 'I am a writer.'

'Oh. There's a writer lives down our road. Now what's his

name . . . ? Ooh . . . Um . . . John, that's it. John, don't know his surname, but he's a writer. Maybe you know him.'

'Possibly.'

'He does stuff for this sort of house magazine the Gas Board has.'

'Oh, really?'

'Says it's very interesting. I dare say you find your writing very interesting . . . ?'

'When it's going well, it's fascinating. When it's going badly, it makes me feel absolutely suicidal.'

'Oh dear. Doesn't sound too much fun. I don't think I could be a writer, you know. Oh, I have these ideas, that's not a problem. But getting them down on paper, that's what I'd find difficult.' The woman looked at Geraldine appraisingly. 'Yes, you know, now you come to mention it, you do *look* like a writer.'

'Oh?'

'Yes, you've got that sort of expression like you're thinking about something else all the time, like you're only half-listening to what's being said to you.'

I could see the noble restraint with which Geraldine just stopped herself from snapping back, 'Given the level of the conversation, can you blame me?'

'Do you write under your own name then?' asked the woman, dragging the conversation even lower.

'Yes.'

'Oh. And tell me, one thing's always interested me about writers . . . Where do you get your ideas from?'

A furrow like a migraine rippled across Geraldine Byers' splendid brow. Knowing her as I did, I understood what pain she was suffering, and tried to extricate myself from my marine insurance broker and go to her rescue. But she waved me away and smiled bravely on at her interlocutor. She was only too aware that it had always been the fate of great artists to be misunderstood and trivialized.

It was fortunate, given the dire state of her social life, that her creative life was going well. *Offshore* had been a surprise winner of that year's Booker Prize, and Geraldine was enjoying her immersion in Penelope Fitzgerald's style.

The winning book was set among houseboats on Battersea Reach and so involved some fascinating research. Geraldine didn't actually go on any boats, but her father had some chums who lived just near there, in Cheyne Walk actually, so she went and had drinks with them a couple of times and asked their views on the denizens of the houseboats. As a writer, she had always found that talking to people who were really 'in the know' was the best possible method of research. And then she fed the research back into her book.

A shudder suddenly ran through *Nostromo*, from fore to aft, and everything lurched sideways. There was no damage, because *Nostromo*'s owner had everything securely battened down, but she rose with a little muscular spasm, and floated free of the mud, as she would for the next six hours, till the tide once again immobilized her.

Roger stood at the head of the companion ladder, leaning against the deck-house, relieved, as always, to be out on deck. The other boat-owners, waving farewells, made their way over the ramshackle series of gangplanks to their own boats. *Sebastian* was moored to the wharf. *Dorchester* lay alongside her, with *Gaston*, *Paula* and *Ironclad* beyond. Roger saw Barry weave and stagger a little as he disappeared down the hatch of *Ironclad*. The old boy was undoubtedly beginning to drink too much.

Battersea Reach melted at the fringes in the first fog of the year. The wash of a passing police duty-boat stirred the minestrone of driftwood, plastic containers and empty bottles that gathered in the angles between the barges. Grubby seagulls ignored the ripples that lifted and lowered them on the oily water.

Roger, obscurely reassured by the gleaming brightwork on the handholds of the companion, went back down into *Nostromo*. The warmth of the Arctic, its regulator damped down to precisely the right level, welcomed him. Through the galley hatch, the pale blue glow of the Calor stove was occulted, as the arm of his wife's Guernsey crossed it. He slumped down on to the blue cushions, which fitted neatly over the fitted-in lockers, and drummed his fingers irresolutely on the brass-bound table-top.

'Think the meeting went well, Dee,' said Roger, never quite as confident of his competency as he appeared, hungry always for reassurance.

Diana was preparing *vol au vents*. She gave him a bleak, heavy-lidded look through the galley hatch, a look more suited to a country house than a boat moored on the Thames. Her resentment of their living as they did was rarely spoken, but it lay between them like a deterrent bolster.

'Bit worried about old Barry, though,' Roger continued.

'He's all right. Seems all right to me.'

'Don't know. I'm not quite sure that he mightn't suddenly do something stupid.'

'Why?'

'Since Zenda left, he's drinking a lot.'

Diana pushed her lank hair off her brow with an unconsidered, patrician gesture. 'What else is there to do stuck on a boat in the middle of London?'

The timbers of *Nostromo* groaned. The weatherboard set up an ominous sighing, every strake straining in sympathy. All along the wharf the mad old boats vocalized their yearning for company.

Barry leant against the doorway into Zenda's quarters. He could hear iron lighters nudging insistently against each other, the dying wail of a hooter, the puttering of a dinghy's Johnson doughtily opposing the tide. The light in the saloon flickered ominously. Due to makeshift wiring, electricity was always a doubtful ally on *Ironclad*.

His eyes slightly bleared with the whisky, he looked across at the impassive television, no more to flicker with her favourite *Dr Kildare* or *Bootsie and Snudge*. Zenda's departure showed all signs of haste. Neat column of shillings and sixpences guarded her bedside table. Her latest *Cliff Richard Weekly* spread, face-down, over her pillow. And across the bed, still moulded a little to the imprint of her form, lay the pale pink sateen trousers, so recently bought from one of the incense-breathing pedlar's stalls on the King's Road. That had been her paradise, her fairground, where she could wander in and out of boutiques, Wearbuy, Luscious Poison, Wearfor, Wearthehell, Who Cares What Mum Thinks?, picking up and discarding the brilliantly-smudged frippery, before sinking into one of the new coffee bars to moustache her lip with the sour froth from the hissing Gaggia machine.

In counterpoint to the trousers, on the floor lay her more habitual grubby anorak, bunched untidily over muddy Wellingtons.

Barry swallowed down sentimentality, like a draught of bitter but necessary medicine, and staggered back across the sodden carpet to his damp sofa and the whisky bottle. The loss of a daughter seemed reasonable justification for a little excess.

The mortuary whiff of river water enveloped him as he drank. The carpet rippled and shifted, before gracefully conceding to the water-level, and slipping out of sight. Barry's shoes filled slowly. The damp crept, discreetly ahead of the dark water surface, up his trousers. The whisky politely shielded him from any unpleasantness.

He did not hear the last despairing death-rattle of its cable as the *Ironclad*'s anchor worked free of the mud with an apologetic sigh. Nor the fusillade of snaps from the overstretched mooring-ropes. Nor did he feel the swaying, crazy, circling lilt of the old, sinking barge, as she swung solemnly out into midstream.

1980

One of Geraldine Byers' most striking qualities – apart, obviously, from her talent – was her honesty. She could perhaps hide her feelings from the outside world, but she could not hide them from herself, she had to confront them. And frequently she confronted them out loud, to me. I would have felt very reticent about writing down some of the confidences I have been privileged to receive from her, were it not for the fact that Geraldine herself has on many occasions urged me to do so. The same unflinching honesty with which she confronts herself is exemplified in her willingness to have that self bared on the page for the common reader, and even to make public something as personal as doubts about her own marriage.

While unable to deny the value of her husband as a lover and as her own private Arts Council, Geraldine Byers could not always suppress a sense of waste when she thought of her marriage. It was all right for George; obviously he benefited enormously from association with one of the finest minds of their generation; but it did seem a little sad that someone like Geraldine had never found a soul-mate who was her intellectual equal.

The history of books, she knew, was littered with stories of great love affairs between writers and, while she could sometimes draw comfort from the image of herself writing valiantly on in the face of domestic incomprehension, she had long felt a need to be part of that more passionate history. She needed the excitement, the danger of a love-affair with a talent as great as her own.

Of course, it would mean being unfaithful to George, but, good heavens, they were just entering the eighties, a decade which she assumed would continue the sexual revolution of the sixties and seventies, and, anyway, her husband must have realized when he took her on that a free spirit like hers was unlikely to be completely fulfilled within the conventional shackles of marriage. Besides, as everyone knows, the restrictions of traditional morality do not apply to artists.

(Also, since – given the law of averages – it was only a matter of time before the Booker Prize was won by a book about adultery in

Hampstead, an affair could be regarded as legitimate and essential research.)

Having reached the decision that such a physical clash of literary Titans was both inevitable and necessary, Geraldine devoted considerable thought to which writer she would bless with the rich gift of her body and self, to which literary biographer she would accord the anecdotal nugget (worth a couple of chapters at the very least) of his subject's affair with the brilliant and torrid Geraldine Byers. (And of course it wouldn't do any harm to Mary Mott's biography of *her* either!)

There was obviously a lot to be said for choosing a poet. Poets tend to praise their mistresses more directly. Novelists have a distressing habit of writing *romans à clef* which disguise their lovers so effectively that nobody recognizes them. Still, Geraldine had not been over-impressed by the poets she had met, back in the days when she worked for *Pivot* and in the years since. Some were grubby, some drank too much, some were gay, all seemed to have far too high an opinion of their own worth. And, though these strictures could apply with equal aptness to many of the novelists she knew, the idea of a novelist still appealed more. Some novelists she had met had a grace, an articulacy, a seriousness about them which very nearly matched her own. And it would be appropriate, after all, for her to conjoin with someone bound to the same harsh discipline as herself. They could empathize with each other's agonies, share the pains of creation during the switchbacks and storms of their great love affair.

The final decision about the identity of the beneficiary of her passion was, like so many of the decisions in Geraldine Byers' life, made for her. In the spring of 1980 she was invited, through a contact she had made while teaching a Creative Writing Day in Godalming, to co-tutor a week's residential course on 'The Novel and How to Write It' for a charitable trust in Norfolk. This centre ran courses throughout the year on such subjects as Pastels, Calligraphy, the Oboe, Poetry, Meditation, Women's Studies and Origami. Its premises were a remote former school in the wilds of the East Anglian countryside. Geraldine had heard of the organization and was flattered by the recognition that its invitation paid to her status as a literary figure.

But the exciting news which the offer contained was the name of her co-tutor. Richmond Gurton was author of four 'significant' novels, each one less compromising and penetrable than its predecessor. His name had been much bandied about in the sixties as a new hope for English literature, and in some circles amazement had been expressed that his third novel, *Blood on the Piston Rings*, had not been shortlisted for the 1973 Booker Prize. Geraldine had actually reviewed his most recent book, *The Cloud of Becoming*, and hailed it as 'a work which transcends the earth-bound manacles of traditional understanding, which forces us to reassess the glib systems of comprehension which most of us all too readily embrace'.

From the moment that she knew he was going to be on the course, Geraldine Byers decided that Richmond Gurton was to be her literary lover.

Though she had been advised that the course style was distinctly casual – denim, track-suits, Guernseys and so on – and she regretfully left behind the knee-breeches she was rather pleased with, Geraldine had still told me to pack her Janet Reger underwear, and to take care that George did not see these preparations.

Boring old fuddy-duddy that I am, I couldn't help asking Geraldine whether she felt any guilt about her decision to cheat on her husband, but after she had very patiently explained to me what an essential part of her development as an artist it was, I saw her point completely. She told me she felt quite tender as she kissed George goodbye, tender as one might towards a small child about to be disillusioned by being told the real identity of Santa Claus.

Once in Norfolk, Geraldine wore the Janet Reger underwear all the time, never sure of the precise moment, but wanting to be ready when the cue came for its erotic opulence to be unveiled.

The concentration required by the course was hard. The two tutors cohabited in the centre with twenty 'participants' (they didn't like being called 'students', and the word which came instinctively to Geraldine's mind, 'punters', was also frowned on). They all cooked together, ate together and held earnest seminars on subjects like 'The Novelist's Sense of Place', 'Character Development' and 'Creative Imagery' together. They also slept together, though not in the sensual meaning of the words; the sexes were segregated into two long dormitories and those who wished to make alternative arrangements were reduced to a few leaky barns and outhouses (a real test of the heat of passion in early December).

The tutors, however, by virtue of their status, were excluded from this ascetic regime and allocated their own private rooms. Geraldine's was, she noted with satisfaction, equipped with a double bed. The scene was perfectly set for the consummation of her great affair of the head.

She got on well with Richmond Gurton. In their mutual seminars and tutorials they soon adjusted to each other's pace, learning when to come in with their own comments, when to hold back and let the other throw in an observation or anecdote. They seemed united in their attitude to the 'participants', a combination of enormous respect for the ambition of these amateurs and a readiness to patronize them at every opportunity. Geraldine thought she made sufficient effort to make her interest in her co-tutor evident, and flattered herself, from a few private looks he had cast in her direction, that Richmond Gurton's libido was also aroused.

However, it was not until the penultimate evening of the week that any positive move was made. They had had a couple of glasses of wine with supper, as was the custom on the course, and Richmond murmured to Geraldine that he wouldn't mind something more to drink.

'Well, I dare say a lot of them'll be going down to the pub, as usual.'

'Yes, but quite honestly I don't want to get cornered again about how to extract someone's hero from a gay brothel without moving from second-person to third-person narration.'

Geraldine laughed softly, acknowledging the reference to the course bore, from whose buttonholing they had both already suffered quite enough. 'Well, look, I've got a bottle of whisky in my room,' she murmured. 'Why don't you drop by and share a glass with me?'

Richmond Gurton winked acquiescence.

'Say half an hour . . . ?'

He nodded.

Geraldine used her half hour to good effect and was showered, hairwashed, perfumed and clean-Janet-Regered by the time she heard the tap on her door. (She also, ever mindful of me, set up a cassette recorder, so that my biography should have as full a record as possible of this important staging-post in her development as an artist. My task in recreating the scene would have been much more difficult without that thoughtful precaution!)

'Come in,' she breathed silkily at the sound of his knock.

They got off to a very good start. At first Richmond sat on the chair by the desk, while Geraldine lounged languidly on the bed, but after a couple of glasses, making some transparent but forgivable excuse about a bad back, he asked if he might join her. Close to, she told me, she was aware of the slightly acrid tang of his masculinity, but did not demur as, still using the alibi of getting his back comfortable, he eased himself closer.

All the while they talked, talked of the things nearest to their hearts: of how rotten publishers were and how deliberately they seemed to inhibit an author's sales by inadequate promotion; of how philistine most critics were, more concerned with clever-clever phrase-making than the recognition of genius; of how blinkered and self-seeking literary award judges were, preferring to advance their own friends than reward obvious merit; generally, of what hell it was being a writer.

This was heady stuff for Geraldine. This was what she had dreamed of, and now that she had it, she realized how parched her soul had been all these years, denied a marriage of true minds to irrigate its intellectual drought. She couldn't help admitting that Richmond's conversation did rather put the hot mumbling of George's foreplay in its place!

On the other hand, as the conversation spiralled on and the level in the whisky bottle descended, Richmond Gurton's foreplay showed no signs of shifting from verbal to physical gear, and towards midnight Geraldine began to think perhaps she would have to act more positively to overcome what must be a congenital shyness on his part. Or more likely than that perhaps, an inability to believe his good fortune, to believe that he actually stood a chance of tasting the superabundance of her charms.

While Richmond had slipped out to have a pee, Geraldine took the opportunity to insert a fresh cassette into the recorder, and on his return changed her approach into more positive mode.

'I think,' she purred, 'that one's writing is so much more fluent when one's emotional needs are being fulfilled . . .'

'Too right. Too right,' Richmond Gurton concurred. 'Obviously one has to have suffered, or one wouldn't be a writer . . .'

'No, of course not.'

'I mean, one must have some kind of central personality defect or one wouldn't bother *writing* about life, one would just get on with *living* it . . .'

'Like *ordinary* people do,' said Geraldine, unable to keep the perjorative intonation out of the word.

'Exactly. I think it's back to old Wordsworth, though . . .'

'It so often is.'

'"Emotion recollected in tranquillity." I think that's true of all writing, not just poetry. Like you say, I write my best when my emotional needs are fulfilled.'

'Yes, yes,' Geraldine sighed.

'I mean, the book I'm writing at the moment is a good example of this . . .'

'So's the one I'm on.'

'Mine's a novel about a life-long atheist and humanist who is suddenly struck down by Faith.'

'I'm doing this allegorical book about a sea-voyage, set in the eighteenth century.'

'Now the thing is, my hero doesn't want the Faith. He tries to resist it.'

'I suppose mine's really in the manner of William Golding. I mean, very different, of course, but perhaps here and there echoes of his style.'

'So it becomes a kind of picaresque quest to lose Faith, a sort of *Pilgrim's Progress* in negative, I suppose you could call it.'

'You see, I take the premise that the sea-voyage is a kind of search for God.'

'And stylistically I'm echoing the rhythms, well, inevitably of the Authorized Version . . .'

'But in my book the "God" *per se* is never defined, so that every reader can kind of attribute . . .'

'But there are influences of other tractarian writers in there, though I don't want to make the language too easy because . . .'

'In my book . . .'

'In my book . . .'

They talked on avidly about their books, both entirely at peace, neither aware of a word the other was saying. After a while, their words slowed, they grew drowsy, and there is silence on the tape.

(By morning the tape had run out, so I have had to rely on Geraldine's description of the next day's conversation. And it is typical of her character that she told me exactly what was said, even though some of it was not perhaps as flattering to her as it might have been!)

They were woken by the morning sun through the curtains, and looked at each other with some surprise.

'Good heavens!' said Richmond Gurton. 'What on earth would any of the punters think if they came in and found us like this?'

'Well, they'd — '

'You know . . .' He started to chuckle. 'They'd think you and I fancied each other!'

He roared with laughter. It was the best joke he had heard for years.

'You mean,' asked Geraldine, rendered incautious by her disbelief, 'you *don't* fancy me?'

'Good Lord, no.'

'You mean I'm not attractive?'

'Never really thought about it.'

'Why not?'

'Well, because you talk about books all the time. I don't want to go to bed with a woman who talks. Least of all about books. All I want from a woman is that she has no brains, she doesn't say a word and she fucks like an angel!'

'Oh,' said Geraldine. 'Oh.' Then, after a pause, 'Do angels fuck . . . actually?'

When she got back from Norfolk, it was very nice to see George. He was delightfully affectionate.

And it was wonderful to be able to get back to her novel.

PLUMBING THE DEPTHS
by
Geraldine Byers
(73)

This is the seventy-third day of our voyage, I believe; but then again my computation could be wrong. The calendar is lost in the confusion of these latitudes, as we young fellows dance around the *maypole* of La Hardcastle. I own that I myself am *épris* with her, and fear I am not alone in this Convulsion of Passion. Mr Cummerbund sighs after her with an unseemly eagerness more fitting to one of the Gallic Race than a gentleman of our own Dear Country. Mr Cibber pays her constant court, doffing his beaver and bowing like a *jack-in-the-box* at a village fair! And poor Mr Winters, though confined to his hutch with a quinsy, sends her hourly *billets-doux*, with the fellow Walker doing service as Ganymede! And who knows what flames her *fluttering eyelashes* may have fanned in the icy heart of Captain Prince! Yet the exquisite torturess herself gives no indication of which way her fancy lies. Nay, rather she blows now hot, now cold, like a plaguey *sou'wester* (See, my Lord, to what good use I have put my studies of Falconer's *Marine Dictionary*!).

Fie, I am sometimes almost tempted to the *blasphemous* opinion that THE ALMIGHTY made a mistake in his PLAN OF CREATION! For would not life have been more civilized for the *male* of the human species if his mind was never shadowed by the thought of doxies, strumpets, harlots, *bona robas* – in short, of women! Your lordship will, I trust, forgive this *lapse* in my religious propriety, but may take it as a yardstick to judge how SORELY I AM TRIED at this time!

My candle gutters low. I must put up this journal and address myself to sleep, which is, God knows, a rare enough visitor to this fetid 'tweendecks *dungeon* in which I am condemned to languish. I will summon the servant Walker for a dose of his paregoric. That, coupled with prayer to THE GOOD LORD WHO MADE ALL, may, I trust, subdue the fevered lusts of my imagination!

(!)

Your lordship will see the pass to which I am brought! An exclamation point, a mere cipher of punctuation, is all that I can offer by way of date! What a to-do! What a confusion! What a thing!

I lie on the bed in my hutch as I write. I have no more candles, and the fellow Walker will bring me none, save at *exorbitant* cost. So I scribble by the thin light that creeps through my louvre. Oh, my lord, I am laid low – felled truly like the Philistine with Samson's Jawbone of an Ass – by a nauseous and pestilential Fever! And yet I

101

partake of more than the Ass's *Jawbone*, for by my behaviour in the last days, I must have appeared to be more than *Half-Ass* myself!

I can scarcely hold my pen, but I *must* be composed. I have undertaken, with MY SAVIOUR as witness, to render unto your lordship a full and proper account of all occurrences and *evenements* of this cursed voyage. And, what though some of my narrative must cast me in the *role* of Simple Simon, dupe or *laughing-stock*, I will not flinch from recording it. Of our poor Humankind, none can afford the *luxury* of SELF-ESTEEM, of being PUFFED-UP WITH VANITY. In the words of Isaiah lxiv. 6 – 'All our righteousnesses are as filthy rags; and we all fade as a leaf.'

To yesterday then, without further ado. We were making good *headway* as we drew near the Tropicks, the masts *listing*, the *shrouds* to *windward* taut, slack those to *leeward*, and the cable of the *mainbrace* swinging out over the *briny deep*. (You see how fluent your servant has become in this outlandish Tarpaulin Tongue!) I was dozing in my hutch, when my slumbers were shattered by a thunderous rain of blows on my door.

'What would you?' I cried, atremble already with fear.

A dreadful voice answered.

'Henry Timbs Button, you are summoned to the Prince's presence!'

In my panic at these terrible words, my thought was of no Prince but the PRINCE OF DARKNESS, for truly I could believe that at my door was an emissary from the D-v-l himself!

'I am divested of all my garments. I cannot come out till I be clothed,' I cried, half-mad with fear.

But the arguments of Modesty carried no weight with my Satanic Summoner. My door was burst down like matchwood, and in burst a figure with a *head from Hades*, huge, 'blood-bolter'd' eyes, 'gory locks', and a mouth whose fangs seemed to drool the blood of innocents. A tarpaulin was forced over my head, and I born away in my shirt, for all the world like a sack of sea-coal to be dumped in a vintner's cellar!

I was thrown down on the hard deck, and heard around me a screeching cacophony, which would not have disgraced the imagination of *Dante*, penning his *Inferno*. Such a squeaking and gibbering! Such a howling and yowling, as if the very cats cried murder on the instrument-makers who *plucked their guts* for fiddle-strings! Around me was the pounding of d-v-lish feet on the wood of the deck, the shouts and screams of licentious voices, mad like *Dervishes* in anticipation of a new soul to torment! Truly, I prayed then as I have never in my life before, to the ONE LIVING GOD! I confessed the long catalogue of my sins, my misdemeanours and my shortcomings, in the terrible certainty that – if I were not already in HELL – then my last hour on this beloved EARTH was come!

The blanket was wrenched off me, and I steeled myself for the *coup-de-grace*. Then, blinking in the light of the lanterns, I was aware of a sea-change in the sounds and sights about me. The screeching of demonic *tongs-and-bones* became the sweet accord of violins. The pounding feet of a myriad *Beelzebubs* gave way to the elegant measure of a *quadrille*. And what I had taken for the screams of *blood-hungry* Imps, I heard now as the laughter of all the passengers on that accursed hulk!

And what, my lord, was the jest at which they roared with such immoderation? It was I! *I was the butt*! I, the focus of their merriment. I, the outlandish entertainment, the *raree-show*, to enliven the diversions of their Tropick Ball.

All about me, through my shame, I saw my fellow-passengers, the men *cap-a-pee* in long coats or uniforms, according to their calling, the ladies airy confections of frills and furbelows. And all laughing, almost to tears, at my discomfiture! Mr Cummerbund stood with the uglier of Miss Hardcastle's half-sisters – though I had sooner have *casting-vote* on a dead-heat in the DERBY STAKES ON EPSOM DOWNS than say which is truly the more hideous! – while Mr Cibber was ardently attendant on the other Monstrosity. And – but, oh, this, my Lord, is what brings me pain, the bitter griping of those Sour Grapes, which must, according to the Prophet Ezekiel, set on edge the Children's Teeth – beside them stood Captain Prince, with his arm around the waist of the fairest woman that ever my eye lighted upon! Yes, Miss Hardcastle! The lovely foundation of my *Castles in Spain*, on which I built so many hopeless Edifices of Phantasy, while I lay *prostrated* in my hutch. The looks which Captain Prince and Miss Hardcastle exchanged *shrivelled*, as the sun's rays through a Mariner's Spyglass, my Foolish Aspirations, and leave me now to daub myself in their ashes, like a Mourning Aboriginal!

I am minded of the words of the Dramatist – let me quote them to you.

> How fad the lot of thofe who love in vain –
> Like Eunuchs fhall they never love again.

But now I must close this journal. I shall bind it fast in canvas, seal it again in oilskin, caulk it with wax, creep up on deck with it at *six bells*, and throw the bloody thing over the *gunwale* into the Inconstant Ocean! We who spend too long at sea become a little crazed, and it is not fair that we should inflict the *bilgewater* that we write on innocent people.

1981

When it was announced that Salman Rushdie had been awarded the 1981 Booker Prize for *Midnight's Children*, Geraldine Byers took an important decision in her writing life. It was no longer possible to be a writer, she announced to me, and hope to get by on inadequate research. Now Magical Realism was in vogue, it became more than ever important to get the Realism right before you started tarting it up with the Magic.

As a result, she told George that she needed a trip to India. It was not just for the research; she also needed to get away because England was beginning to depress her so much. She cited the Brixton riots, Toxteth, Belfast, unemployment moving up towards the three million mark. George did not stop to ask in what way any of these disasters impinged on his wife's life, but did as he was told and made the relevant bookings. Just after Christmas, they set off together from Heathrow. Geraldine took *Tristram Shandy* and *The Tin Drum* to read on the plane.

They did what everyone else does when they go to India – saw the Taj Mahal and the other tourist sights, were shocked by the poverty, and came back with a particularly virulent and tenacious tummy-bug.

But the trip was a success; not only did it help Geraldine's research, it also had an effect on their marriage.

One night in a hotel in Delhi, before the tummy-bug struck, she reported to me that after a particularly memorable bout of sweaty love-making, they had lain together, sated and relaxed.

'You know, George,' Geraldine had said, 'I do wish you took more interest in literature.'

'Ah,' he had said. It was not the first time in his marriage that this subject had come up.

'I mean, you don't show any interest in my work . . .'

'Oh, now that's not fair, Geraldine. Why are we here now? It wasn't my idea to come to India. We're here directly because of your work.'

'Yes, but I mean, you never show any interest in my Work-in-Progress.'

'That's because you never tell me anything about it.'

'I never tell you anything about it because I know you wouldn't understand.'

'How do you know I wouldn't understand if you never tell me anything about it?' George had asked, reasonably enough.

'Well . . . Well . . . If I did, how would you respond?'

'I don't know, do I, because you never do.'

'No, but . . . I mean, say I asked you to read a bit of what I was working on at a given time, would you do it . . . ?'

'Of course I would. I'd feel privileged to do it.'

Geraldine had smiled contentedly. Every now and then George did have the knack of saying exactly the right thing. She felt magnanimous towards him. 'Very well then, I'll let you read some of my next manuscript . . . when I feel ready.'

'Oh, thank you, Geraldine. I'd be very interested. You see, I've been thinking I'd quite like to have a go at writing myself.'

'George . . .' She had laughed gently at the incongruity of the idea and rumpled his hair.

There had been a silence. Geraldine felt swimmingly contented. In a moment George would reach his arm across her body, draw her to him and make delicious love to her again.

'Geraldine . . .'

'Hm?'

'If I do start to show more of an interest in your work . . .'

'Yes?'

'Will you start to take more of an interest in mine . . . ?'

'George! In chemicals? Take an interest in chemicals? Oh, really . . .'

She had had to laugh. He'd been a bit hurt at the time, but soon bounced back. She felt in some way the conversation had brought them closer. Of course, he was never going to be absolutely the right man for her, there was no way the massive intellectual chasm between them could ever be narrowed, but the marriage really was quite workable in some ways.

In spite of the tummy-bug, she felt revived when she returned from India, and settled down with great energy to work on her new novel, *Midnight's Noses*. When she had completed Book One, she came to a natural break in the process of composition and, as she had promised, offered the manuscript to her husband to read.

George, properly sensible of the honour, accepted with alacrity.

MIDNIGHT'S NOSES
by
Geraldine Byers
BING, BONG

Now the pace hots up: now the countdown urges the clockhands forward till they stand entwined, the one shielding the other, erect, ready to explode with the jism of history. Mountbatten's time-bomb is ticking, its English time more reliable, more regular, than Bombay time. And I wait, restless to emerge into my own story; to take my rightful place at the centre of my narrative; to pacify the rumbling gargantuan appetite of my ego; to be the crux of so many lines, the fixed point at which such a plethora of individual histories converge.

(Are we getting there? asks Farida. Is something going to happen soon? I smile over my typewriter, scratching the magic itch of my magnificent nose.)

. . . There are two days to go to the handing over of power and the bing-bong moment of my potential birth. On the telephone Prince Shaman orders tiny curry tartlets, fragrant fruit-juices, sparkling waters and some nice cocktail nibbles. 'They must be here on time. No, there is no argument. This is more important than the orders for the foreign sahibs' farewell parties.' . . . The pendulous cucumber of his nose, and potentially my nose, dangles, an inflamed sporran between his legs.

Now in the godown everything goes up in flames. A hundred and sixty-three years snap, crackle and pop away into smoke signals with the milk of independence gushing over them. 'Ay! Ay!' shouts Dr Patel as the whole world goes mad and hysteria snatches at the throat of India. Pinocchio noses lengthen at the tall stories of the Hindu wise-men, other noses are blown and drip, regular as clockwork, dropping jewels of snot on to the perforated handkerchiefs of all my potential ancestors.

. . . Thirty-six hours to go, thirty-five, thirty-four, thirty-three . . .

(This is good, says Farida. Now we are getting somewhere. Maybe, I reply infuriatingly, maybe, unwilling yet to commit myself.)

And my potential mother, bathed, oiled, refined, sanded with sandalwood, buffed in the buff, varnished with vanishing-cream, french-polished, glances at the photograph of Edwina Mountbatten in *The Times of India* and lifts a languorous hand to pop a slice of Mountbattenburg cake under the great portcullis of her nose. She smoothes her sari against her seed-hungry, me-hungry belly, and looks down at her tiny mirror-decorated slippers.

Twelve hours to go. Deep in the intestinal labyrinth of his nervousness, kamikaze butterflies batter themselves against the stomach wall of my potential father's turbulent frame. Vertiginious, heaving, bubbling craters of fear swell and pop on the soup-surface of his serenity, as the newest date on the calendar draws nearer, the red-letter day whose digits are already washed in blood after the flood-gate release of amniotic fluid until now imprisoned by the membranes of history.

Five hours now. Four. Three. The marquees are set, the bunting garlanded from poles, coir matting laid over the pampered grass of the Palace, hard boards of the dance floor spirit-levelled for the high spirits to come. The conch shell that will sound the Last Post of

Empire misses the last post and has to be sent by special delivery, a wavering bicycle threading the fabric of New Delhi, pulling tight the drawstring ruffles of the temple curtain soon to be torn in two.

Two hours.

(We must be nearly there now, grumbles Farida. Yes, yes, I soothe her. See, the guests are already arriving.)

An hour and a half to go. Now the spitoons in the Palace are slashed with jets of betel-juice, aureoles of missed spit spreading out of their interplanetary maps, as the stars move on ill-favoured collision course and astrologers wet their loin-cloths in anxiety. The old men spit on in spite into the spitoon . . . all but one, the Prince, my potential father, whose grotesque vegetable-marrow of a Ganesh-trunk blocks his aim and leaves the red fluid dripping snottily from its proboscis.

. . . Dancing. Wild cocktail stomping to the ting of temple bells and the crumhorn grumble of conches, while the conchies who will not dance for religious reasons sit this one out, wall-flowers against the fly-paper wallpaper. 'I say, old chap . . . Goodness . . . Pardon me . . . oops . . . this is the gentlemen's excuse-me, isn't it?' Is it? 'Ay! Ay!' scream Dr Aziz and Professor Godbole. 'All is disaster! One of us is in the wrong book!' Or the right one, as the Constituent Assembly is stirred in the melting-pot of history to a new consistency and reassembled.

(Oh, get on with it, says Farida. You have spent so long getting to this point. Now at last something is going to happen, can't you speed it up a little? No, I say smugly, you must wait. Everyone must wait.)

Noses? What of noses? Noses sniff in the Punjab, noses blow against the brick-built fortresses along the line that will soon dissect the Siamese twins of Pakistan and India. Huffing and puffing to blow the house down, cowing the three little forbidden pigs inside and pigging the sacred cows in the fields around them. Another huff. A mighty puff from the cannon-mouth nostrils, and the fortress shifts, lifts, rises, falls, shatters and crumbles. Alas! Alas! . . . it is not the first – and I fear will not be the last fortress that has been either won – or lost by NOSES.

(Haven't your potential father and mother met *yet*? asks Farida. Oh yes, I reply complacently, knowing that I alone hold the reins of timing, oh yes.)

. . . They dance. Their noses touch, a collision of orbiting fleshly meteors whose reverberation threatens to shake down all the fruit from the Great Tree of Knowledge, the Yggdrasil of Mountbatten's India, to wake the sleeping eagle, to bruise the heel of the lagging serpent and drown all history in the rotten windfalls of dominion.

Jawaharlal Nehru rises from the thunderbox, wipes himself for the last time as a British subject and moves stately to the Constituent

Assembly, mouthing the words of his tryst with destiny. The two noses are delicately lifted aside, as surgeons slide back the foreskin of a trepanned skull, for the lips to conjoin in the kiss that will be the sealing-wax on my letter of introduction to futurity. To Whom It May Concern.

The first bing sounds. The first bong. Bing . . . bong . . . bing . . . bong, beating the tattoo of destiny, the retreat of the Raj, the reveille of two sleeping giants . . . it is midnight at last.

The current is reversed, the poles change, the attraction of the Brobdingnagian noses turns to repulsion, the faces are forced apart. My potential father's nose drops stunned to tickle the ground like an overweight dachshund's dangler. My potential mother's nose quivers in anguish, is cataracted with tears that blur her eyes, as she turns and stumbles blindly off, catching one tiny foot against the edge of a saffron and green carpet and losing one tiny, mirror-decorated slipper in her haste. This is not the moment when the long incubation of my potential being is to be started in the feathered warmth beneath the Great Chicken of history. I will have to wait a little longer.

(Farida. Wake up, Farida! I am just getting to the interesting bit . . .)

George took the manuscript with him on a week's business trip to Brazil. (Geraldine needed a break after her efforts and was happy to relinquish the precious document; she spent the time he was away at a health farm. This was quite convenient, actually, because it gave me a chance to spring-clean the house!) As soon as George returned, hollow-eyed with jet-lag, before I had even had a chance to offer him a drink, Geraldine demanded, 'Right, what did you think?'

'Well . . .'

'Come on. I'm not afraid of criticism. I can take it.'

'All right.' He hesitated. 'To be quite honest, I'm afraid I didn't like it much.'

I could see how his words cut her to the quick and could understand the sharpness of her reaction. 'I see! Well, that's the last time I show you any of my work! I might have known all you would do would be to criticize!'

'No, no, please. Listen, Geraldine, what I'm saying is, I mean, some of it's obviously jolly good. It's very clever, it must have taken a lot of time, clearly a lot of effort gone into it, but, um, I just don't think it's my sort of book.'

'No, well, I agree it hasn't got lots of bodies and car chases and glib readability and — '

'No, Geraldine, I just mean that that sort of book doesn't sort of . . . suit my imagination.'

'What there is of it,' she snapped, unforgiving.

He tried to mollify her. 'Some bits were fine. There's a bit round Page 57 that was absolutely straightforward, I could understand every word.'

'Oh,' she said, taking out a pencil and scribbling a note, 'I can change that.'

'It's just . . . I don't know, Geraldine, the style seems a bit . . . over-inflated.'

'I'll have you know, that sort of style is very popular at the moment. *Midnight's Children* is selling amazingly well. Everyone in Hampstead's bought a copy.'

'But have they all read it?'

'All my friends have started it.'

'How many of them have finished it?'

'Well, I . . . Well . . .' She evaded his eye. 'Most of them are still reading it . . . they don't want to, sort of, rush it . . .'

'I see.'

Geraldine slumped angrily on to a sofa. 'You've really upset me now. Honestly, George, it doesn't take long, does it? You come back from a week away and within five minutes you've upset me. You're just so bloody insensitive.'

'I'm sorry, love, but you asked my opinion . . .'

'If that's the kind of opinion you have, I'll know better than to ask again then, won't I? I mean, what do you know about literature? What gives you the right to criticize a brilliant novel?'

'I don't know. My reactions are very simple. I sort of go for what I find readable, and I sort of tend to prefer that to what I find unreadable.'

'God,' Geraldine said in exasperation, 'simple is right. Simplistic might be more accurate. Sometimes, George, you are just so *crass*!'

'Yes. Maybe. I'm sorry.' He hung his head. 'Shall we have a drink?'

'I thought you'd never ask. I'll have a glass of white wine, Mary.'

While I was pouring the drinks, George said, 'This trip to Brazil was just amazing. The things that are being done out there . . . Can I just tell you about the — ?'

'Oh, do shut up, George!' Geraldine shouted. She was still deeply wounded by his insensitivity. I held her drink out to her. She snatched it from my hand, then reconsidered, took the bottle too, and stumped upstairs with it to the spare room.

'What did I do wrong?' George asked me in bewilderment.

I tried to explain, but it wasn't easy. Only another genius could really have explained Geraldine's behaviour.

1982

After the announcement that Thomas Keneally had won the 1982 Booker Prize with *Schindler's Ark*, Geraldine Byers spent some weeks in the London Library, researching the atrocities of the Holocaust.

She subsequently graduated to the British Library, and continued her researches there for some weeks.

Then she suddenly came to the decision that she was essentially a fiction writer, the integrity of whose imaginative genius could only be coarsened by the effort of getting all her facts right.

So she decided to give herself a sabbatical, and do no more writing until after the announcement of the 1983 Booker Prize winner.

Instead, she became for a while a political creature. She spent a lot of time at Hampstead dinner parties agreeing with people that the Falklands war had been a disgusting thing for Britain to get involved in, that it was just the last twitching of an outdated imperialism. She also spent most of an afternoon at Greenham Common (she would have stayed longer, but she was going to the theatre that evening).

1983

When the 1983 Booker Prize was awarded to J. M. Coetzee for *The Life and Times of Michael K*, it was clear that Geraldine's research was going to involve more foreign travel. She remembered with a shudder the Great Writer's Block of 1974, a horror story still frequently relived for the entertainment of rapt Hampstead dinner parties. In retrospect, she was more inclined to accept Virginia Rawson's point about lack of preparation being a contributory factor in that ghastly episode and, warned by the Nadine Gordimer experience, was not prepared to risk starting another book about South Africa until she had been there.

George was unavailable for the trip that year. He seemed to be busier than ever with whatever it was he did in chemicals and travelling a great deal, particularly to Scandinavia and South America. He also announced rather simplistically that he disapproved of the South African régime and didn't feel one should support it by spending holidays there.

'But that's the whole point,' said Geraldine, misunderstood yet again. 'One does disapprove of it. Deeply, deeply. It's for that very reason that one has to go out there, to see for oneself what's happening, get some first-hand experience. And really, George, you ought to know me better by now than to imagine that what I want to go out there for is a holiday. It will be a trip of relentless hard work, a gruelling fact-finding mission.'

'Yes, of course, love,' George apologized. 'Well, look, I suppose, if you've got your heart set on it, you'd better go to some travel agent and fix up a safari or whatever it is you do.'

'Not a safari,' Geraldine said pityingly. 'And actually I've had a much better idea than a travel agent. Daddy's got lots of former business colleagues out in South Africa.'

'He would have, wouldn't he?'

'I beg your pardon, George?' Geraldine asked sharply.

He quickly covered the lapse. 'That is, I mean, your father has such a wide international circle of friends, it's no surprise that some of them live in South Africa.'

'That's better,' said Geraldine, not completely forgiving.

Her father, still remarkably sprightly as he approached his eightieth birthday, was delighted to oblige ('as you know, absolutely anything I can do for you, my old bread-and-butter pudding, you only have to ask'). He did have lots of chums living in South Africa, but he thought the most suitable for Geraldine's purposes would be Bobo and Gretta, who had a large farm near Pretoria. 'Absolute bricks, both of them. Soul of generosity, they'll see you all right, my old Eccles cake. Lived there for years, know everything about the place.'

'I think they should know,' said Geraldine seriously, 'before I arrive, that I am not a supporter of the régime in their country, or of *apartheid*, and that I will be out there to research the iniquities of the system.'

'Sure that'll be no problem, my old Swiss bun. I won't bother them with that beforehand, though. You can make it all clear when you get out there.'

'Well, all right, Daddy, if you think that's best . . .'

'You take my word for it, my old chocolate truffle.'

Not only did Mr Byers make all the arrangements for her visit, he also insisted on paying for her flights. Geraldine did sometimes think about how fortunate she was, how much she had been pampered and protected all her life, how much she had been made to feel she belonged, that for her all was for the best in the best of all possible worlds.

But every time this thought came to her, she was reminded of its reverse side. As she often and ruefully reminded me, there was no rose without a thorn, and her privileged position was a positive disadvantage in her self-imposed creative mission. Almost all of the Booker Prize winners seemed to be novels about dislocation, dispossession, not fitting in, not belonging. It didn't make the task easy for someone who had grown up with her advantages. God, it was hell being a writer.

Bobo and Gretta proved to be quite as hospitable as Mr Byers had promised. The farm was set in astonishingly beautiful countryside, there was a lot of socializing, lots of swimming and riding, and Geraldine didn't really get many chances to ask about the conditions of the blacks, or 'blecks' as Bobo called them.

But of course her writer's antennae were always alert, picking up every nuance and vibration of the unfamiliar civilization into which she had been thrust. The trouble was, she didn't actually see many 'blecks', so it was hard to form very definite impressions. Of course there were lots of servants round Bobo and Gretta's estate, but they all seemed very efficient and, so far as one could tell, perfectly content with their lot. No one talked about rioting or police brutality. Geraldine began to suspect that the horror stories of *apartheid* which figured so largely in the British press were just more examples of media exaggeration. It was hard to see people as generous as Bobo and Gretta in the role of racist imperialists, a lot easier just to accept their hospitality with grace, to relax and enjoy herself. Which is what she did.

But, though she had temporarily put the political resonances of her new book on one side, she felt confident that she was assimilating some very useful information about the topography of South Africa.

There was also, as she confessed to me afterwards with her usual frankness, another distraction for her. Bobo and Gretta had a twenty-five-year-old son, Dirk, huge, blond and sport-obsessed. He claimed never to have read a book in his life and his conversation rarely rose above the level of jokes against the 'blecks', but Geraldine could not deny that she was attracted to him. Maybe something like that was what she needed at this stage of her life. The more sensational English newspapers were full that year of stories about forty-year-old actresses and 'toy-boys'; perhaps a relationship of that sort could have a rejuvenating effect on the genius of Geraldine Byers.

It was ridiculous, of course. Dirk had no intellect, but maybe it was time that she abandoned herself to a purely animal encounter. It would probably be a very useful experience for her as a writer. There had to be a short story in it at least. She even started making a few notes, full of words and phrases like 'unalloyed physical gratification', 'rampant sexuality', 'throbbing beast' and 'stallion'.

It was for these reasons, she told me, that she let Dirk seduce her (if 'seduce' is not too refined a word to describe the process). He was bowled over by his good fortune, saying that this was 'a bit of a turn-up for Dirk's Donger'. He instantly pounced on and penetrated her with no foreplay at all, completing the whole transaction in less than thirty seconds. Geraldine found the experience somewhat painful; still, she supposed, there must be an element of pain in an encounter of 'unalloyed physical gratification'. And perhaps hoping for them both to achieve 'unalloyed physical gratification' the first time had been unrealistic.

As a result, she allowed further encounters, to see if better results could be achieved, but the improvement, if any, was minimal. The 'donger' still seemed to 'dong' distressingly quickly, though this never prompted any apology from its owner. It was as if Dirk wasn't *trying* to gratify her. Such a concept was almost unthinkable to a woman of the eighties; surely all men had by now been made aware of the subtle triggering necessary to release the flood-gates of physical pleasure in a woman. However, as quick bang followed quick bang, with 'donger' jokes taking the place of endearments, Geraldine was made to face the painful truth: that Dirk was no respecter of women, in fact a totally insensitive chauvinist of the old school. So the experience was not ultimately a happy one and rather soured the last week of her stay with Bobo and Gretta. And, the final shame for a liberated woman of the eighties, she actually found she felt *guilty* about what she'd done.

She tried to block it from her mind with writing, and was relieved to think that at least there wouldn't be any sex in her new novel.

THE LIFE AND WALKS OF SINDY L.
by
G. M. Byers

After she escaped from the guards around the compound, L. walked through the night in the direction which she hoped led to Sodafontein. At last, dizzy with exhaustion, she crept under a culvert and fell immediately asleep.

It rained during the night. In the morning the rain had stopped, but her ragged clothes were damp, her belly rumbling its emptiness. She started to walk, avoiding the roads, for fear of soldiers or roadblocks, keeping to the high ground. The one shoe made her movements uneven, so she took it off and threw it into a clump of veld-grass.

The hunger did not abate. It griped at her belly, but the sodden grassland offered nothing for her to eat. After two or three hours she sat down against the post of a barbed wire fence and went through her pockets. It was a hopeless but necessary ritual. She knew she would find nothing that was edible.

There was a ten-rand note left from the money her father had given her, the green card which was almost certainly out of date by now, and, screwed up in their brown envelope, the dried pumpkin seeds. The seeds were all that she had brought with her from the compound. She cupped them in her hands and raised them to her face. They still carried the sweet scent of the pumpkin flesh and aroused memories of a certain midnight which she quickly suppressed. All that was behind her now. She must walk on to Sodafontein. If she could find the farm with the garden where her father had been happy, then perhaps she would be happy as well.

For a moment she considered eating the pumpkin seeds. There must be a little goodness in them, maybe enough to give her energy for a couple more hours' walking. She could soften them in her mouth before swallowing them down. But she decided against it. The hard husks would irritate her belly. And if she kept the seeds, maybe one day she would be able to plant them and raise pumpkins of her own. But they would be just ordinary pumpkins. There would be no magic in them.

Revived by her rest, she walked on, but soon began to flag again. The sun was high overhead. It had quickly dried out the wet grass and its haze distorted the thick bush of the horizon.

She did not know what would happen next. This did not worry her; not knowing what would happen next had been the story of her life. No doubt in time she would think of something to do; or someone would appear to tell her what to do. Meanwhile, the best thing seemed to be to keep walking.

Her ears were singing with exhaustion and hunger, and she almost walked straight into the stationary convoy. Just in time she stopped herself and lay quickly down behind a bush. A smell of frying eggs teased her empty stomach. She peered cautiously through the branches of the bush.

The reason why the column had stopped was a burnt-out truck, lying sideways across the road. A thin plume of smoke still rose from the blackened cab. Soldiers from the convoy stood around, looking at it without much urgency.

Near to L., two soldiers in camouflage uniforms crouched over a makeshift fire with their egg-pan.

'Doesn't matter too much if we're delayed,' said the first soldier. 'We can still obey our orders. They're not going to get far. They've nowhere to hide.'

'But we don't know exactly who we're looking for, do we?' said the second soldier.

The first soldier shrugged. 'Doesn't matter too much. We round up all the women. Put them all in the camp. Then we look at them one by one, at our leisure. See which one it fits. Take the shoehorn to them, if necessary.'

The second soldier laughed coarsely. L. shuffled backwards on her belly, down the hill. There was nothing for her here. When she was in the dry valley, shielded by hills from the convoy, she stood up and went on walking. She walked all day, all night, and all the following day. Then she found a small, dry cave, crawled into it, and fell asleep.

1984

'So . . .' Hawthorne Rackham rubbed his hands together, relishing the situation. 'Here we all are again. How quickly the years come round. It seems only a few weeks back that we were settling down to judge the 1983 Humphrey Halliwell Prize.'

'Mind you, last year's didn't get any publicity either,' Lilian Grimshaw griped. 'I mean, nothing has changed since I won with *Trugs in the Orchard*. You'd think that — '

'Sorry, Lilian, rather a lot to do this afternoon. Better get on.'

Lilian Grimshaw snorted and sat back in her chair. Hawthorne Rackham beamed at Frances Hood, 'Well, perhaps we should ask the Secretary to remind us of the six books on the shortlist . . .'

The composition of the BNA committee meeting that afternoon at the Dilettante Club had not changed significantly since 1976. The rules about how long members should serve had always been hazy and there was a general lethargic feeling that, once on the committee, unless individuals felt particularly strongly about leaving or unless they flounced out in resignation (as occasionally happened), they were on for life.

Elfrida Elton had been on for life, but unfortunately her life had ended in 1977, and she had been replaced by an indistinguishable literary aristocrat called Elvira Eglington. J. Marthwaite Bentley had resigned on a point of principle when the BNA finally decided to give the 1979 Public Lending Right Act its support (support which, since the measure was by then on the statute book, was totally irrelevant), but after a few years without excuses for not actually getting on with some writing, he had reinstated himself. Margot Lockyer's mother was still not well, so she wasn't present; Stanley Ribble still claimed to be in the throes of a work crisis; but Wanda Grosely, Lilian Grimshaw, Geraldine Byers and of course Frances Hood seemed to be fixtures. Hawthorne Rackham said at every Annual General Meeting that he really thought it was about time he stepped down as Chairman and if anyone felt moved to take over the mantle, he would be more than happy to withdraw . . . But no one ever did feel moved, so Hawthorne Rackham seemed quite content to stay on as Chairman.

At practically every committee meeting since 1976 there had been discussions about the administration and judging of the Humphrey Halliwell Prize. Sub-committees had been set up, reports written and studied. Resolutions had been passed that, whatever else happened, the BNA should ensure that the final decision was not left to its own committee. Outside judges should be brought in, a panel of critics invited, objectivity should be attained at whatever cost.

And every year the Humphrey Halliwell Prize had ended up being judged by the BNA committee without any outside interference.

'I'll read the titles of the shortlisted books,' said Frances Hood in her quiet, precise voice. '*A Stray Thistledown* by Margot Lockyer; *Hotel du Lac* by Anita Brookner; *Rapture, Rupture* by Stanley Ribble; *Flaubert's Parrot* by Julian Barnes; *Sweet Aspect of Princes* by Merrily Rogers; and *Two Steps Back* by Julian Scutt.'

The titles were greeted by little mumbles of appreciation and dissent. It had taken many hours of argument to arrive at the shortlist. A great many other books had been proposed and rejected, frequently on the grounds that no one had read them, and committee members had fought tenaciously for their own particular favourites. But the shortlist had eventually been hacked out and copies of it sent with covering letters by Frances Hood to a selection of Literary Editors, all of whom had ignored them. At the end of that afternoon's deliberations, the name of the winner would be rushed off in hastily-written letters by Frances Hood to the same selection of Literary Editors, who would once again ignore them.

Geraldine's own views on the shortlist, which she had gone through with me before she left for the meeting, were extremely definite. She thought it was a scandal that books by committee members were allowed even to be considered, and would continue to think so until she finally published another book herself. So she would fight vehemently against the Margot Lockyer and the Stanley Ribble. The Julian Scutt she thought was illiterate drivel and, though she had enjoyed *Flaubert's Parrot*, she considered it a bit lightweight to win a prize for the Best Novel of the Year. Merrily Rogers' book had quite a lot of charm and was clever, but Geraldine had met the author, a television presenter, at a dinner party where they had both turned up in the same Next dress, so that ruled her out.

Which left the Anita Brookner as, for Geraldine's money, really the only serious contender in the field. *Hotel du Lac* had recently won the Booker Prize and Geraldine thought that connection could only help in raising publicity for the BNA award. A paperback edition bearing the words 'Winner of the Booker and Humphrey Halliwell Prizes' would do no harm at all to the Association's profile.

But, publicity considerations aside, Geraldine did like *Hotel du Lac* enormously. As she investigated the book with a view to starting

117

her next novel, it seemed to strike more and more chords in her own life. Geraldine Byers felt herself, in her forties, to be part of that generation of unnoticed women, the ones who drifted round on the edge of crowds, unconsidered by the busy world. She wrapped self-pity snugly round her like a woollen cloak. No one looking at her would guess the passions that beat in her breast; no one know of the brief, all too bitterly brief, interlude of doomed happiness she had enjoyed with a hopelessly younger man in South Africa; no one understand the heartache she had been caused by her decision to relinquish her claims and let him get on with his own life. Geraldine Byers had taken to drifting round London on her own, drinking solitary cups of coffee in museum and gallery cafeterias, mourning for her life. She felt Anita Brookner spoke to her directly, with understanding, woman to woman.

Hotel du Lac must win the Humphrey Halliwell Prize.

'Right, so let's get started,' said Hawthorne Rackham. 'Well, I think we can rule out the Anita Brookner straight away.'

'What!' Geraldine almost screamed.

'It won the Booker Prize,' the Chairman explained.

'I know, but what's that got to do with it?'

'Well,' he continued patiently, 'for one thing that means she's had quite enough publicity already, not to mention money. And, for another thing, we don't want people to think the BNA just copies what the Booker lot do. The BNA does have its own identity, which must be preserved at all costs. *And* we're doing this for nothing,' he added righteously. 'The Booker judges get paid, you know.'

'But surely what we're here to do is to decide which is the best novel of the year? That should be our only consideration.'

Hawthorne Rackham shook his head in avuncular reproof. 'Oh, now, Geraldine, you know there are a lot of other considerations we have to take into account.'

'But, Hawthorne — '

'Now I'm afraid we can't take too long on this. Look, let's put it to the vote.' He glanced across at Frances Hood, indicating that he was moving into official Chairman mode. 'I propose that the committee agrees to exclude Anita Brookner's *Hotel du Lac* from further discussion. Those in favour?'

The majority was in favour. The shortlist was down to five.

'I think, actually,' J. Marthwaite Bentley began, 'we should rule out the Julian Barnes for the same reason.'

'Tarred with the Booker Prize brush again, you mean? It was on their shortlist.'

'Exactly, Mr Chairman.' J. Marthwaite Bentley's pipe puffed out an all-enveloping cloud of smoke.

'Well, it would certainly save time if we only had four books to consider. Would the committee be in favour of our putting it to the vote?'

'Sorry, is that a resolution?' asked Frances Hood, anxious as ever to get the record correct for her minutes.

'What do you mean?'

'Well, are you going to put to the vote the resolution that the committee is in favour of putting it to the vote that we rule out the Julian Barnes?'

'No, I was thinking more in terms of just putting it to the vote that we rule out the Julian Barnes.'

'Oh, fine. Sorry, just wanted to be clear on that.'

'Right. So . . . I propose that we exclude Julian Barnes' *Flaubert's Parrot* from further consideration for this year's Humphrey Halliwell Prize. Those in favour . . .?'

Out went the Julian Barnes. Geraldine didn't feel so strongly about that, but she was still seething about the exclusion of the Anita Brookner.

'Good, down to four,' said Hawthorne Rackham with jovial satisfaction. 'We *are* getting through them, aren't we?'

'Yes. I think there is one point worth mentioning,' said Frances Hood, who, as well as acting as Secretary and Treasurer, took on the duties of Membership Secretary. 'Which is that neither Anita Brookner nor Julian Barnes are even members of the BNA!'

'Thank you very much for pointing that out.' The Chairman chuckled. 'Make us feel a bit better about eliminating them, eh? Now . . . what's going to be the best way to proceed? What we could do is just all vote on the remaining four and see if we have an outright winner . . .?'

'Oh, I think we ought to *discuss* them first,' said Wanda Grosely, for whom reaching the decision as to which book had won was insignificant, compared to the pleasure of talking about them all at inordinate length.

'Yes, I suppose perhaps we should. Maybe you'd like to kick off by giving us your views, Wanda?'

She nestled her substantial bulk comfortably into her chair in gleeful anticipation of a long monologue. 'Well, I think the Julian Scutt is absolute balderdash. Hardly literate, I don't know how it got on to the shortlist.'

'I happen to think that, at his best, Julian Scutt is a very fine writer,' said Lilian Grimshaw combatively. 'I mean, this book may be dreadful, but I don't think we can dismiss a writer of his stature in such a cavalier way.'

'Well, Lilian, that is a comment on the standards that you — '

'One at a time, one at a time, please,' the Chairman interposed. 'All get a chance to talk in time. On you go, Wanda.'

'*Sweet Aspect of Princes* does have a certain glib charm, but it's the kind of story that has been written considerably better by other authors. I mean, I have no wish to blow my own trumpet, but I think my own *Trim the Sail Yarely* was a much more successful venture into similar territory. And I think we should be here to encourage proper novelists, not television presenters who do a little writing in their spare time. So we're down to the Ribble and the Lockyer . . . Well, I thought Margot's *Floating Leaves* was far and away the best of last year's shortlist and still can't really see why it didn't win.'

'It was a very fine book,' the Chairman agreed judiciously, 'a much better book in fact than the one we're discussing this afternoon. *A Stray Thistledown* seems to me to be a marked step backwards for dear Margot.'

'Yes, but she is a writer of considerable eminence, and I feel that our awarding the prize to the author of *Floating Leaves* would be a very appropriate recognition of that eminence.'

'But dammit, woman,' protested J. Marthwaite Bentley, who prided himself on his occasional bluntness, '*Floating Leaves* is irrelevant to this afternoon's discussion. We're talking about *A Stray Thistledown*, and what you have to ask yourself is whether *A Stray Thistledown* is a better book than Stanley's *Rapture, Rupture*. Which clearly it isn't.'

'No,' said Wanda, 'I agree *Rapture, Rupture* is Stanley's best book to date, but the fact remains that his attendance record at committee meetings is quite appalling . . .'

'That's true,' Hawthorne Rackham agreed gravely.

'. . . and if we give him the Humphrey Halliwell we're as good as condoning his habit of not turning up.'

Everyone nodded agreement. She had made a good point.

'Well, thank you very much. Cogent and economical as ever, Wanda.' The Chairman turned to favour his oldest committee member with a gracious smile. 'Perhaps we could hear your views, Elvira . . . ?'

They heard Elvira Eglington's views. At considerable length. Then they heard Lilian Grimshaw's views, J. Marthwaite Bentley's views and Geraldine Byers' views. So that she didn't feel excluded and sulk (as she had been known to do), Frances Hood was asked to give her views, even though she didn't have any voting rights in the final judgement of the prize. Not to be left out, Hawthorne Rackham then let them hear his views. The consensus at the end of all these views seemed to be that they all thought *Two Steps Back* by Julian Scutt was dreadful, they all disliked Merrily Rogers because she was famous, and the only two books really in contention were *A Stray Thistledown* by Margot Lockyer and *Rapture, Rupture* by Stanley Ribble.

'Well, this time I think we're going to have to put it to the vote.'

There were a few remonstrances from those who wanted to keep talking, but eventually they accepted the validity of their Chairman's suggestion. They voted. Frances Hood, voteless herself, counted the votes. Hawthorne Rackham, J. Marthwaite Bentley and Lilian Grimshaw backed Margot Lockyer; Wanda Grosely, Elfrida Eglington and Geraldine Byers went for Stanley Ribble.

Discussion followed about whether the Chairman was entitled to an extra casting vote according to the BNA constitution, but foundered after a quarter of an hour or so, as such discussions usually did, when somebody remembered that the BNA didn't have a constitution.

The Chairman suggested that committee members should put forward a few further arguments in favour of their choices and then they should vote again to see if anyone had been persuaded to change his or her mind. The further arguments were put forward, and the vote retaken. Elfrida Eglington had been persuaded to vote for *A Stray Thistledown*, but unfortunately J. Marthwaite Bentley had now come round to the merits of *Rapture, Rupture*.

Impasse. They continued to discuss the books, but no one was prepared to shift allegiance again. Those who had stayed firm for the second vote were determined to continue resolute, and those who had changed their minds once didn't want to look indecisive by changing them again.

'Well, look,' said the ever-resourceful Hawthorne Rackham, who had been through these hoops a few times before, 'let's move on to an alternative system where we each have two votes.'

'Can we use both for the same book?' asked J. Marthwaite Bentley.

'No. For two different books.'

'Sort of first and second?' asked Lilian Grimshaw.

'No, two votes of equal value. And we'll see who gets most votes that way.'

Once the new rules had been made clear to everyone, the vote was taken. Margot Lockyer and Stanley Ribble still got three votes each. The personal animus against Merrily Rogers (for being famous and attractive and seen regularly on the nation's television screens) was such that she only gained one vote.

Which was how Julian Scutt's *Two Steps Back* came to be awarded the British Novelists' Association's Humphrey Halliwell Prize for the Best Novel of 1984. (The announcement of the award, incidentally, got no press coverage at all.)

After the excitements and responsibilities of judging, Geraldine Byers was quite relieved to get back to work on her own book.

HOTEL DU BAL
by
Geraldine Byers

Through the curtains another perfect day was revealed: the mountain, trickled with creamy snow like the chocolate mousse of the night before, looked as close as the balcony rail; boats scudded across the glassy surface of the lake, fewer boats now, because the season was ending; by the landing stage many of the smaller ones were beached, upturned for the winter; on the hotel lawns waiters in clean white jackets collected the garden chairs and tables and brought them in under the glass awning. This was a land of propriety, where none of the accoutrements of summer dared commit the solecism of being left out for the winter.

Ellen Payn poised her pen over the open exercise book on the eremitical table at which she sat, willing herself back to the second chapter of *Mistress of True Melancholy*, the latest romantic novel of her *alter ego*, Cindia Nash. She proposed to use the book as a buffer, which would channel her concentration away from the events that had brought her to the Hotel du Bal.

But her mind resisted this marshalling. Her hand instead reached automatically to the stall of neatly stacked hotel notepaper, on which she was soon at work, her book forgotten.

'My darling Charles (she wrote),
'Well, I have arrived, another strange, faded, prim tourist in a muted cardigan, told by everyone in London that I should have a break from everything, and meekly doing as I am told. The hotel is half empty. I have seen a few elderly ladies, nursing secret griefs in the salon, and engaged in conversation with one *declassé* Belgian Comptesse about the relative merits of Geneva and Lucerne. M. Gruber, the owner, shows a properly detached solicitousness for my welfare, though clearly I am no more to him than a foreign name in the hotel register. Otherwise, interrupted only by the occasional *"Oui, Mam'selle"* from the waiters, I inhabit my own silence.

'You still fill my thoughts. I cannot rid my mind of the expression on your face when I left you that midnight. Am I fanciful to have read disappointment into it? Or was it just relief that I was offering you the chance to get on with your own life? I wonder what you are doing now . . .'

She had been the one to make the break. It had had to be like that. The magic between them had been perishable; better to undo

122

the spell while it was still there than to wait for it to shrivel into bickering. She had felt a little death when they had parted, but knew the separation would soon be a *fait accompli*, he moving away from her, she immobile. Though not the most efficient method of eloignment, it did, however, ensure that the chasm between them would grow, slowly but inexorably, wider. And that his pain would diminish as hers increased.

She knew exactly how Charles would have reacted: shaken his head in disbelief as he watched her departing silhouette, checked on his watch that midnight was really past, then started slowly back to Holland Park and the wife whom Ellen never saw, whom he claimed did not exist, but whose reality she could not doubt. He would have slept uneasily, nurturing his anguish, but woken in the morning to the anonymous urgencies of the day's work. And, through the clouds of loss, small pencils of light would gradually have infiltrated. The ease of return to the placid waters of his former life, the relief at the end of deceptions, would have begun immediately to heal his scars. Without the sight of her to set him back, the pace of his recovery would have accelerated. He had always been the one who had less to lose.

Ellen had been forced into exile. It could have been anywhere, but the Hotel du Bal, traditionally and self-effacingly run by the Gruber family, was as good a place as another in which to lick one's wounds. Here she would walk, eat meals in the echoing dining room, attended by impassive waiters, and try to eclipse her own world with the imaginary world she must create for *Mistress of True Melancholy*. Soon, she mused gloomily, it would be time to change out of her dour cardigan into an unobtrusively well-cut suit, and face the ordeal of dinner.

'Oh, my darling (she wrote), you will never know exactly how much you meant, and how much you will always mean to me. Perhaps that is just as well. Better that only one of us should be aware of the true enormity of our separation. I can only wish you happiness. In your case, that is a reasonable wish; you are capable of attaining it. Never insult my intelligence by wishing me the same. For people like me, lasting happiness has never been an option. If it ever came to me, I would be unable to cope with it.

'I miss you, and will always miss you, but that is my problem, not yours.'

She signed her name with a practised stroke of the pen, capped it, and sealed the letter in an envelope bearing the Hotel du Bal crest. She felt

1985

'Hello, my name's Susannah Franks. I'm calling from Abrams & Willis.'

'Oh.' Geraldine looked at the telephone with some surprise. It was such a long time since she had had any communication with her publishers, she had almost forgotten their existence. 'And what do you do at Abrams & Willis?'

'I've just moved from the Publicity Department, now I'm an editor.'

'But in the past Sidney Parrott always — '

'Afraid poor old Sidney had a stroke last year.'

'I am sorry. Is he . . . ?'

'Well, he's still alive, but he won't be coming back to work again.'

'Oh dear. I should drop him a note or something.'

'Wouldn't bother. He's in some home and apparently more or less completely gaga.'

'Oh. Oh, well . . .' Geraldine couldn't really claim to be that upset. Not one of the great publishing relationships, Geraldine Byers and Sidney Parrott. He'd read the manuscript of *Pale Cast of Thought* in 1967, suggested a change of title, then thought better of it and stuck with the original; otherwise the book had been printed exactly as she delivered it; early in 1974 he had claimed to have read what she'd written of *The Ball of Calcutta*, which he'd found 'interesting, but difficult to judge without seeing the rest of it'; and that was it. Hardly Scott Fitzgerald and Maxwell Perkins.

So Sidney Parrott was quickly dismissed from her mind. What was much more interesting was that his replacement was making contact. Perhaps, Geraldine wondered, with firmer editorial support, with someone nagging at her to keep going at her work, being slightly tyrannical even, her progress towards winning the Booker Prize might be speeded up a little.

'Anyway,' Susannah Franks was saying, 'I was going through some of Sidney's filing cabinets and I came across a copy-edited manuscript of something called *Pale Cast of Thought*.'

'Ah yes,' said Geraldine fondly. 'Did you enjoy it?'

'What?'

'Did you enjoy reading it?'

'I haven't read it.'

'Oh.'

'No, it's just . . . I was about to chuck it out and then I thought perhaps I should check with you. Some authors like to keep that kind of thing.'

'Yes, I would certainly like it back, thank you,' said Geraldine with a degree of coldness. 'Manuscripts do have a certain value, you know.'

'Well, some of them, yes,' Susannah Franks agreed with a laugh. 'Still, I can understand that you might like to have it as a kind of memento.'

'A memento of what?'

'Of the days when you used to be a writer.'

'I still am a writer,' said Geraldine magnificently.

'Oh, I assumed you'd given up.'

'What on earth gave you that idea?'

'Well, you don't seem to have published anything since 1968 . . . Unless of course you've been published by another house . . . Or under a pseudonym . . .'

'No, no.'

'So it has been just the one book . . . ?'

'Volume isn't everything,' said Geraldine coldly.

'No, no, of course not. But you are actually working on something?'

'Certainly.'

'Oh.'

'I'm sure you'd like to hear what it is.'

'Well, I do actually have rather a lot of calls to make this morning and — '

'It's a substantial work of literary fiction.'

'Really?'

'Yes. Have you read *The Bone People*?'

'Sorry?'

'The winner of this year's Booker Prize.'

'Oh yeah. Right. The one where those feminist weirdos pranced up to collect the award. Yes, with you. Hear it's a dog.'

'I'm sorry?'

'The book. I hear it's an absolute dog.'

'Oh.'

'Anyway, Geraldine, look, must dash. Maybe we should meet up one day . . . ? Lunch at the Groucho or something . . . ?'

'Well, I'd love to, but the thing is, I'm leaving to go abroad in a couple of days.'

'Oh. Where to?'

'New Zealand.'

'Good luck. Rather you than me. I gather it's all pretty much like Orpington, New Zealand.'

'Oh.'

'Well, sounds like we'll have to make it after you get back.'

'Yes. Um, unless you happen to be free this evening . . .'

'What?'

'My husband and I are giving a little party, you know, just drinks and nibbles, but you'd be most welcome if you were free.'

'Oh, well, I'm not quite sure what I'll be doing, but I'll see if I can drop by. Give me the address.'

In the flesh Susannah Franks looked about eleven. Apart from a huge Katherine Hamnett 'STAY ALIVE IN 85' T-shirt, she appeared to have nothing on but a pair of thick black tights and trainers. George offered her a drink, she said a glass of white wine would be 'brilliant'.

'Mary, could you get Susannah a white wine?' he asked, and when I brought it to her, she and George were deep in conversation. Geraldine was busy doing her hostess bit and attending to her other guests, but each time she looked across to them, the girl and her husband still seemed to be talking.

'Oh dear,' I heard her murmur to Virginia Rawson, 'looks as if that poor kid's cornered.'

'What?'

'George giving her all the dreary details of the chemical industry, I'm afraid.'

'Oh, well, actually, it's quite interesting what he's doing at the moment, because — '

Geraldine put her hand on her friend's shoulder. 'Really, Virginia dear, you don't have to pretend with me. It's very sweet of you, but we do both know that George, whatever his good qualities, is just about the most boring creature on God's earth. Come on, let's go and rescue the poor child.'

She sailed across to them. 'Now, George, you mustn't monopolize Susannah. I'm sure she wants to meet some other people.'

'No, don't worry. What your husband was saying was very interesting.'

Geraldine let out a tinkling laugh at that idea, then said, 'Virginia, this is my new editor, Susannah Franks. Could I introduce Virginia Rawson . . . ?'

Susannah Franks' mouth dropped open. 'Not *the* Virginia Rawson. The writer.'

Virginia shrugged. 'I suppose so.'

'Gosh. Well, look, if ever you have the tiniest doubt about your current publisher, give me a bell, won't you?'

'All working very well where I am at the moment.'

'That's a bugger. Never mind, worth asking. George and I were just talking about AIDS.'

'Oh, really?' said Geraldine.

'Yes, I've commissioned a couple of AIDS books. Going to be very big next year, AIDS books.'

'Oh.'

'Latest thing I heard, they reckon it started in Africa.'

'AIDS?'

'Yes.'

Susannah laughed. 'Still, needn't worry about that – unless you happen to have been screwing around in Africa, eh?'

Geraldine cleared her throat and gave out a pale smile. 'About the book I'm working on, the one I mentioned on the phone . . .'

Her editor didn't appear to have heard her. 'Made a big difference to the image of the dear old condom, though, hasn't it?'

'What?'

'AIDS. I've never liked condoms much myself, always feel as if I'm being fucked by an oven-ready chicken, but they are going to be big.'

'Condoms?' asked Geraldine faintly.

'Right. I've commissioned a couple of condom books. Going to be very big next year, condom books.'

'Ah.'

'Well, it's sex, isn't it? Always room for more fucking books.'

'More fucking books about what?'

'No, more *fucking* books. Books about fucking.'

'Oh.'

'Always go well. I mean, they have to be vaguely respectable, not just smut . . . you know, have a doctor's name on the jacket. No, get a *Joy of Sex* on your list and you're home and dry. 'Cause you can keep updating it, you see. *More Joy of Sex, Joy of Sex – The Sequel, Joy of Sex Rides Again, Joy of Sex – The Second Coming* or, in these post-AIDS days, *The Slightly Muted Joy of Safe Sex.*'

'Yes,' said Geraldine. 'Yes, I see.'

'So there'll be plenty of fucking books next year . . . And BMX books . . . and Sinclair C5 books possibly, though I'm not so sure about that . . . oh, and Green books . . .'

'Green books?'

'You know, environmental . . .'

'Oh,' said Geraldine blankly.

'Just talking to your husband about that.'

'About what?'

'Effect of chemicals on the environment.'

'Oh.'

'Well, it is his subject, isn't it?'

'Is it?'

Susannah Franks laughed. 'Very good. Very good.'

'Um . . .' Geraldine asked tentatively, 'do Abrams & Willis still publish fiction at all?'

'Oh, sure. Yeah. But we've diversified quite a lot in the last few years.'

'Evidently. Let me tell you a little bit about the book I'm working on, Susannah . . .'

'What? Oh. Um . . .'

'I'm well under way on a draft, but now I'm really getting to the stage where I need to check some things out . . . which is why I'm off to New Zealand . . . I mean, I don't actually know any of the Maori language, so I'll want to bone up on that – Oh, *bone* up, rather good that, little unintentional joke there. Anyway, I'm sure you'll be interested to know about the *way* I work. I always have a large supply of green Venus 2B pencils and . . .'

It was always a pleasure for me to see Geraldine Byers, the writer, up and running on her favourite subject. And how fascinating it must be, I thought as I went round refilling glasses, for a new editor to hear so much detail about one of her authors' working methods.

THE BONE HEADS
by
Geri Byers
whenua pika pa buka
morehu reed –
morehit kan mak ua pukapuka mate
13
The Woman By Her Own

She walks down the street. The asphalt stays beneath her soles.
People smile at her, perhaps in pity.
Thoughts slide in her charcoal brain.
She does a hop and a skip, and a strange little dance.
And people go on looking at her.
And who can blame them.

. . .

She stalks fish, creeping, prone to flounder. Her ankles sing with the wetness of the water. She circles marram grass, muddy-footed through the sloshing of the ngaio marsh. She moves toe foot ankle shin calf knee thigh bottom, half-slipping half-sliding on the silt. Raises barbed harpoon over milky mud. Wherethehell have all the berloody fish gorn?

129

I talk to myself a lot. Well, I have to. Nobody else listens.

Only one sandal left in the dust. Footprints halfshoed halfunshod must have led from the dance-imploded scene. Aue. The indentations of her knobknuckled foot might fit the sandal.

Why do I look so straaaaange?
(And spell sooo pecooooliaaaarly, come to that?)
Lump-breasted, hump-shouldered, stump-fingered.
Generally thought to be pretty odd.
Good subject for the singing scalpel of the moneypunched plastic-surgeon.
Ugly like my one whole sister in the sisterhood, but unlike the other half, the glitter-haired, rag-clad, carnation-pupilled pretty one.
Right old chewinggumboot I am, still can't do much about it, can you.

. . .

> Long thin drool of cloudcloak
> And high sky bluedrifted
> Hangs away and gets wet
> In the rain.

> Birddrop dropping, puffbird,
> Thermal-lifted, feather-floated
> With little beady eyes
> Open;
> Solitary woman hangs around:
> Hoping to understand something
> Anything.

. . .

Her boat is moored in Whangkomputa, twenty-foot clinker-built, full of holes. She mourns keening as she snatches at the outboard cord. Fool, fool, unsandalled fool, disqualified from sandalfitting by imploded toenail. Kia ora kiri te kanawa kiki dee.

. . .

Dissolve.
Geddonwithit. Berloodywellgeddonwithit.
Now Wakowako and Kikabukit join her for a meal in Whaiwheror-when, chomping puha and pikopiko curls. They wipe satisfied skincovered hands on jeans.

She felt sick.

Things were always like this.

Just get things sorted out, and they start to go wrong.

Right man, wrong time. Right sandal, wrong foot.

Enough to make you bloody spit.

She spat.

Bloodily.

Wikabaskit came to say Gidday and joined them playing the holestrung guitar. Desiderata on wall. Wine drunk. Drunk wine. Sheeit. Words burbled guitar-bounced from mouthholes.

> *Hika ra dika ra*
> *Doka*
> *Mus ra napa klok.*

The lullaby was clouded breath on a winter pane.

> *Wi wil i win ki.*

(. . . a tuneless brrkbrrkbrrk of finger-stuffed nostrils underscores the sschplop! of percussion and kerplung! of freezedried clingfilmwrapped oooaaahs from the splurging burgeoning intestinal subtext of reverberating titipoos . . .)

. . .

'What you reckon then?'

  'Hard to say, really.'

'You've put your finger on it there.'

  'Nice of you to say so.'

'This is it, though, isn't it?'

  'Yes.'

'This is it.'

. . .

Writing.

In italics. Why not, after all?

We must be getting to the end now, the book's core. About time, don't yer reckon, mate? Too berloody right.

Do you realize, if people didn't experryment with it, the novel form might die out like the dinasores or the chukapukawhangas. So that's why books like this or say Finnegan's Wake have to be written – not to be read, but just so that writers will be scared witless about what can be done to language and, in self-defence, go back to writing proper books better.

. . .

AAAAAHIEEEE! AAAAAHIEEEE! Effoff.

Right on, old kiwi fruit.

No fun being ugly with the wrong-sized foot.

And still she tries to pick up her notwanted feet, dance the threaded, spinning reel.

> *O what a thing*
> *The moon is*
> *Sort of white and round,*
> *Except when it isn't –*
> *Always seen,*
> *Unless cloud gets in the way.*

Hands clasp to join the dance, circling round the dawning of a new today.

LINGA LONGA – KI NA TONGA

Translation of Peculiar Words and Phrases

17   E ba gum = Think nothing of it

29   Hi ho sil va = Good on you, mate

57   O u chi ti chi ti bang bang = Apparently much of New Zealand is very like Orpington

84   Haere ti day in gon ti mara = Well, how about that then?

307 Hoi ti toi ti = a rather unpleasant marine univalve

481 Kan ui tit = Is this edible?

599 Hau nau brau nkow = Isn't it about time we had a material symbol for the life force in this book?

742 Uara poopoo = God, sometimes you're so infantile

875 Ka min ta da ga din mord = The tide goes in and out

983 Buka Buka lossa ma zuma = Good heavens, do you really mean that you can win prizes for stuff like this?

1986

Geraldine was at a loss to understand why Mo had included George in his invitation. It was perfectly reasonable for him to ask *her* out for lunch at the Caprice. Even if there was really no sexual element in his motivation (and she told me wryly that she found that rather hard to believe), the two of them could obviously have an interesting time together, mutually discussing books, her reporting progress on her latest novel, and so on. Yes, all that would be extremely pleasant and civilized. But why George should be invited as well, to bring the conversation down from the Olympian heights of literary discussion to his more mundane level, she could not imagine.

Briefly she floated the idea to me that perhaps Mo was after some kind of confrontation, that he wanted the three of them together when he told George to his face about his undying love for her, told George how he had tried to forget her over the years but found it impossible, told George that this was the ultimatum, that now it was over to Geraldine and she would have to choose between them. But the scenario didn't seem right. Such a confrontation was not Mo's style. No, she concluded with a degree of reluctance, she would just have to wait till the day came to find out the reason for the double invitation.

(She knew, however, that the meeting would be a significant one and generously, without my having to prompt her, suggested that she should take a small cassette recorder in her handbag, so that her biography should not be deprived of all the details of the encounter!)

Geraldine dressed carefully that morning in a dark business suit with massive shoulder pads, and spent a long time blending the colours of eye-shadow on her lids. (Unsatisfied with the early results, she sent me out twice to buy some new colours!) Whatever Mo's motivation for arranging the meeting, she was determined that he should not be unaware of what he was missing. George, needless to say, would be wearing a pin-striped suit.

When they arrived at the Caprice, she saw that Mo was also in a suit, though of more exotic cut than her husband's. He wore large red-framed glasses and a flamboyant bow-tie. His hair was even thinner, his baldness deeply tanned. He had put on quite a lot of weight, but prosperity exuded from him like aftershave.

He ordered *kirs royales* for all three of them, then waved to Lord Weidenfeld, who was just entering the restaurant with one of the Longford clan. He acknowledged their reciprocal waves before turning back to his guests.

'Well, been quite an exciting year,' he said with a self-satisfied grin.

'Certainly has,' George agreed.

'Has it?' asked Geraldine, perplexed. 'In what way particularly? Are you talking about Wole Soyinka getting the Nobel Prize for Literature?'

'No, love. The takeovers,' her husband explained.

She must have still looked blank, because Mo asked, 'Haven't you heard what's been going on at P & L?'

'Well, no, not really.'

'Don't you read *The Bookseller*? Don't you read the papers?'

'Well, of course I do a bit, but I've been very busy working on a new book recently.'

'Then let me put you in the picture. As you know, things have been going pretty well at P & L in the last few years.'

'I sort of got that impression, yes.'

'So well that six months ago I bought up Abrams & Willis.'

'Oh goodness, I didn't know that. So you're my publisher now?'

'Well, I suppose I would be if you ever published anything, yes.'

Geraldine was hurt. That kind of cheap gibe was really quite unnecessary. Still, she comforted herself, Mo would sing to a different tune when she won the Booker Prize. And this time she really did feel confident that she was on the right track. It was such a relief that Kingsley Amis had won that year, a pleasant change to have a winner who actually told stories. She was having great fun rewriting her novel in the new style.

'Anyway, after Abrams & Willis, I heard that the Enchiridion Group was in trouble.'

'Enchiridion Group?' Geraldine echoed faintly.

'Fischer & Gotlieb, Stoney & Stoney, Cranbourne Educational, March Hare Computer Publications and Leveret Children's Books.'

'I didn't know those were all in the same group.'

'Well, they are – were, perhaps I should say. They're all still in the same group, except that it's a rather larger group now. A group known as P & L.'

'You mean you've taken them over, too?'

'Exactly, Geraldine. Glad the message has got through at last.'

She didn't like his tone. She had forgotten how patronizing Mo could be. Why was she meant to know all these irrelevant details about takeovers? Next thing he'd start maundering on about the Big Bang or whatever it was, like all those dreary stockbrokers she kept meeting at dinner parties. What had that kind of nonsense to do with Geraldine Byers? She was a writer, not a financial correspondent.

'And what gives on the American front, Maurice?' asked George.

Mo crossed his fingers and winked elaborately. 'Let's just say nothing's gone wrong so far. No, actually very promising indeed. I think that could all be sewn up in a couple of months.'

'What, are you buying up an American publisher too, Mo?'

He winced. 'Maurice. Please.'

'Oh, very well. Maurice.'

'In answer to your question, though, yes, I may well be buying up an American publisher.' He giggled and mimed to the waiter to bring another round of *kirs royales*. 'But only a little one.'

'And what sort of books will your huge conglomerate be publishing, M-Maurice?'

'Profitable ones,' he replied with a wolfish grin. He lapsed into self-satisfied silence for a moment before asking, 'How is the book going, actually?'

'Well, I'm just getting to a very fascinating stage,' Geraldine began. 'The sort of story outline is vividly clear to me and I'm now getting down to the — '

'No, sorry, I was talking to George.'

'What!'

'Have to take an interest in my authors, you know.'

Geraldine turned the full napalm of her displeasure on her husband. 'What is this, George?'

He shrugged apologetically. 'I did tell you about it, love, but I don't think you really took it in.' She was silent; her eyes continued their work of defoliation. 'Geraldine, you remember how interested Susannah got in my work . . .'

'Chemicals,' she murmured, with all the contempt the word deserved.

'Yes. Well, she kept trying to persuade me to write a book about it, and I kept saying I didn't think I could, and she said I really had a public duty to do so, and eventually I agreed.'

'I see. And what is this great work of art going to be?' she asked with withering scorn. 'A block-busting saga? A sort of Arthur Hailey set in the chemical industry, full of cardboard characters and gratuitous sex, tailor-made to be a tatty American mini-series?'

'Oh, no, I leave that sort of thing to you, love.'

'What!' she demanded, scandalized.

'I mean, I leave *fiction* to you. My book's going to be *non-fiction*.'

'Oh, I see.' She relaxed slightly. Her hegemony over the world

135

of creative literature was not, after all, to be challenged. 'A school text-book, is it? *Chemistry for O-Level*, that kind of thing?'

'Hardly,' said Mo, with a guffaw. 'No, it's going to be a Green book.'

Geraldine recalled that she had once heard Susannah Franks use that expression, but she couldn't for the life of her remember what it meant.

'You know, environmental,' Mo explained. 'We're all very excited about it at P & L.'

'Oh.'

'I mean, we're just so lucky to have found an author like George.'

'Really?'

'You see, the trouble is that the whole Green thing has still got an image problem. People still think a Green book is going to be written by some bearded weirdo and published on his own wood-block printing press. So suddenly for P & L – or I suppose technically for Abrams & Willis – to have got an author who is internationally recognized as an expert on chemicals, someone who has actually initiated the whole movement to introduce safety standards in the use of chemicals, who's been a leading light in the campaign to save the Ozone Layer and combating the Greenhouse Effect.'

'This is George we're talking about, is it?' she asked faintly.

'Well, of course it is. Come on, Geraldine love, I know you're a bit dozy — '

'Dozy?'

'Yes, but even you must know what your own husband does for a living.'

'Um. Yes. Yes, of course. It's just that George hasn't said a great deal about his book . . . you know, he doesn't like to talk about Work-in-Progress.'

'You mean you've been talking so much about your Work-in-Progress he hasn't had a chance to get a word in.'

Geraldine didn't dignify that offensive crack with a response. She suddenly realized that Mo wasn't really a very nice person at all. It was difficult to imagine how she'd ever managed to spend any length of time with him.

'Anyway . . .' Mo raised his glass. 'Here's to the book, George. Good luck with it. We're all confident it's going to be one of next year's big sellers.'

George was properly diffident and self-depreciating. Geraldine flashed him a withering look under her multi-coloured eyelids.

'No, it's terrific,' Mo continued. 'A rare combination for a publisher to get – a backer and an author you actually want, all in one. I mean, occasionally people offer to back you on the condition that you publish their dreary memoirs, but this is almost unprecedented. And someone who's really committed to the arts, as well.'

'What?' Geraldine was confused. 'Backer? Someone who's really committed to the arts? What is all this? What are you talking about? Who are you talking about?'

'Well, obviously I'm talking about George.'

'What about George?'

'The fact that George helped me set up P & L in the first place.'

'I beg your pardon?'

'Oh, come on, Geraldine, you know. Back when I was living in Notting Hill . . .' She would have preferred him to say when *we* were living in Notting Hill. '. . . and I wanted to set up a publishing business and I asked you if you'd put some money into it and you turned me down, so then I asked George . . .'

'Why?'

'He was the only other person I'd met who'd got any money. Remember, I met him down at your fascist parents' place in Gloucestershire. And, as I recall, I wasn't very polite to him then, so all the more credit to him for agreeing to back me.' Mo looked across at George with something approaching awe. 'You know, you married a most remarkable man, Geraldine.'

It was at this point that she remembered the tape was still running and, under the guise of getting out a handkerchief, reached into her handbag to switch the machine off. So I have no record of what was said during the rest of the meal. And, for once surprisingly unco-operative, Geraldine did not volunteer to recreate the remainder of their conversation for me.

She was still furious when she got back to Hampstead, and of course I could forgive the things she said to me when I heard what had happened to her. She felt bruised, used, deceived and insulted. When she had finished listing my shortcomings, she stormed up to her work-room and sat down in front of the word processor George had bought her earlier in the year.

She must write. As ever, writing was the only thing that could block from her mind the memory of the appalling way she had been treated.

THE OLD FARTS
by
Geraldine Byers
Seven – Barry

'Always go to the lavatory before you leave the house in the morning. Just sit there. Don't worry how long you sit there. Don't go out until something happens.'

'Could be there all day in my case.'

'No, it'll work. Take my word for it.'

Cliff looked dubiously into his half-pint of beer. Having borne it proudly like a battle-scar for over forty years, he regarded constipation as his own special subject, one on which he didn't welcome advice, but it was too early in the day to take issue with Frank.

There was a silence. There were often silences in the back room of the Crown, as the old farts paced the conversation, rationing their observations to last a good few years yet.

'Morning, Frank. Cliff. What'll it be?'

Barry could see their glasses were hardly touched, but still observed the ritual greeting. The offer declined, he went to buy his own half of Gwynfar bitter. The silence remained unbroken until he lowered his considerable bulk into the chair beside Cliff.

'Bottoms up,' he said heartily, but only tilted the glass a fraction to take his first cautious sip of the day. The other two wet their lips in acknowledgement.

Cliff grimaced. 'Beer doesn't taste like it used to these days.'

Barry also screwed up his face. 'God, I hate beer,' he said.

'Talking about constipation, we were,' Frank confided, not wishing to exclude the newcomer from the previous conversation.

'Oh yes?'

Cliff was even less keen to have the topic pursued now that there was a third party to contribute unwanted advice, but fortunately Barry didn't pick up his cue.

Frank wasn't content to let the subject go. 'That was at the bottom of what happened to old Phil. Bowel cancer. I remember him sitting in here. You remember him sitting in here. Couple of weeks later, he was gone.'

Cliff was not going to stand for this. His relationship with his constipation was a close one, and not unaffectionate. He did not like to hear it libelled. 'I think you're making a rather large assumption there, to link constipation with bowel cancer. What do you base that on?'

This was answered by the appropriate silence. Frank could not summon any evidence to support his assertion and, since neither of the others had any medical knowledge, Cliff got his way, and the subject quietly expired.

Barry eyed the juke-box in the corner uneasily. 'God, I hate juke-boxes,' he said.

Dewi, the landlord of the Crown, had promised it was only put there while the front bar was being refurbished, but Barry remained unconvinced. Its mere presence threatened the peaceful exclusivity of the back room, and talk of refurbishment was ominous. It would be easy for the blight of steel chairs and glass-topped tables to spread from the front bar, forcing out the dark oak, the smoke-yellowed wallpaper and the high shelves with their rows of miniatures. Dewi was not really to be trusted. He was not a proper old fart, not yet secure in the crustiness of his age. He kept trying to act younger than he was. It showed in his hideous blue denim jackets. It could easily show in his refurbishments.

'God, I hate Dewi,' said Barry.

'He's a type.' Frank spoke as if this explained everything. 'A very Welsh type. There are a lot like him in Wales.'

'God, I hate Wales,' said Barry. It was true. He had been born in Wales and hated it then. His hatred had only abated when he lived in Hampstead for a few years, but that was because he always hated where he lived more than where he didn't live. As soon as he'd moved back, Wales had reclaimed its rightful place at the top of his hating list.

'How're the girls then?' Cliff was asking. After his victory over the constipation, he felt magnanimous. The health of Barry's three daughters was of no interest to him, but the occasional automatic cordiality was another of the back room conventions.

'Not so bad. Little one's moping. Two big ones are the same as ever.'

'What's wrong with the little one?'

Barry shrugged. 'Love-life?'

That seemed a reasonable explanation to the other two. Reasonable, but not interesting. Though the old farts were all married, they had long since ceased to have any emotional engagement with women. Women, they had concluded, were basically mad, and love only made them madder.

'Women,' said Frank, shaking his head.

'God, I hate women,' said Barry.

The other two nodded, reasserting another article of their faith.

'I'll drink to that.'

All three glasses were raised to their lips, as the door burst open. Two girls stood there, swaying slightly. Their hair was dyed, not like the old farts' wives' hair in colours that hair might just conceivably be by nature, but in garish fluorescents. Their clothes were black, punctiliously ripped, cross-rigged with chains. Unaware of the disapproving glares over three beer glasses, one of the girls said, 'Got any beermats in here?'

In unison three beer glasses descended to cover three beermats.

'Only there's this competition,' the second girl said. 'Charmaine Breweries. Called *If The Shoe Fits*. Launch for their new lager. Big cash prizes. Income for life. Lots of other goodies. Match up the right pictures on the beermats to win.'

'Oh.'

She seemed not to notice the coldness of Frank's monosyllable. 'So wondered if we could check yours . . .'

'There are no beermats in here,' said Cliff with withering precision, '*except* the ones we are using.'

'Oh.' The girl lingered hopefully. Her friend gave up first. 'Come on, we're not going to get anything out of these old farts.'

They left, closing the door with unnecessary force.

'God, I hate young people,' said Barry.

'Yes,' said Frank. 'Always hoping to get something for nothing.'

'Yes. In my young day,' said Cliff, 'we had to work for everything we got. Work bloody hard.'

The three old farts nodded agreement at this palpable untruth.

Another silence followed. 'God,' said Barry eventually, 'I hate everything.'

1987

Geraldine told George that she really needed the fortnight in Egypt. It wasn't just for the Booker Book, though obviously Penelope Lively's win with *Moon Tiger* made a research trip essential. Geraldine had always had a sneaking feeling that her early effort in the P. H. Newby manner had been handicapped by the fact that she'd never been to Egypt, and she did not want to make the same mistake again.

But it wasn't just for research; she also needed a break because of her emotional state. The Stock Market Crash of 19 October had set up shock-waves all over the world, but had also reverberated in the life of Geraldine Byers. Her father, on hearing the news of what had happened to his remaining investments, had dropped dead of a heart attack. It was the end of an era. The house in Gloucestershire would have to be sold to pay off Mr Byers' debts; some other little girl would soon lie in Geraldine's bedroom looking up at the Cinderella frieze; and, in the short-term, her mother was virtually penniless. It was therefore essential that George should pay for his wife and mother-in-law to have a fortnight's holiday in Egypt.

Geraldine wouldn't be sorry to get away. She had tried to settle down to her Penelope Lively book, but her concentration wasn't good. Partly, it was the delayed shock of bereavement, but also it was because she kept being distracted by the telephone. I tried to protect her by answering it myself as much as possible, but Geraldine was cursed with the writer's occupational curiosity and found it hard not to pick up the receiver the minute it rang.

Frequently the caller was Susannah Franks, incongruously imagining that Geraldine would be interested by news of some further sales record broken by George's *Green Book of Chemical Responsibility*.

But Susannah wasn't the only distraction. Now that his book was riding high in the best-sellers list, journalists and television producers kept ringing the Hampstead house to try and arrange interviews with George. Geraldine was as polite to them as she found it possible to be, but she couldn't help letting them know that it was very disturbing for a creative writer to be constantly interrupted. She was, as it happened, she would then tell them, just starting work on a major new novel and, though she did not normally like to put her artistic flow at risk by talking about Work-in-Progress, she would be prepared to make an exception in this particular case. To her amazement (and to mine when she told me about it!) none of the journalists or television producers seemed to want to take advantage of this heaven-sent opportunity to get an exclusive interview with Geraldine Byers.

I could understand exactly why she needed to get away.

And of course George (with some help from me in cooking meals and that kind of thing) could look after himself. He always had done in the past.

A very strange thing happened the afternoon after I had driven Geraldine and Mrs Byers to Heathrow. It was a Tuesday, I remember, and I had intended to go back to my flat and do a bit of tidying (my work for Geraldine was so absorbing that I didn't get back to my own place as much as I should have done!). But then my conscience got the better of me. Geraldine had made so many phone calls in the few days before her departure, I knew I really should make a start on transcribing the tapes. So I went back to the Hampstead house to start work.

I had been transcribing away for an hour or so with the headphones on, when I suddenly became aware that I was not alone in the house. I could hear noises of movement from upstairs.

Fearfully, I crept towards the source of the sound, which proved to be Geraldine and George's bedroom. I stood outside the closed door and listened.

The first sound I heard was a gentle pop, almost like that of a champagne bottle being opened.

Then I heard a voice, which was unmistakably George's, saying, 'Exciting change, isn't it, having one of our Tuesday afternoons in my house rather than yours.'

A woman giggled and a familiar voice said, 'After fifteen years, maybe we need the stimulus of new surroundings . . .'

George's voice joined in the giggling. 'There hasn't been a single Tuesday for the last fifteen years when I've needed any more stimulus than what I can see in front of me, Virginia.'

The giggling continued, then changed in tone to something more rhythmic, almost as if the two of them were both having an attack of asthma at the same time.

I couldn't imagine what was going on, but I decided perhaps I would go back to my flat, after all.

(I didn't mention this strange incident to Geraldine, but I have written it down here in her biography. When she reads through this draft of the book, perhaps she'll be able to explain it to me!)

Geraldine enjoyed her Nile cruise, though she did find the constant company of her mother a little wearing. When she got back to England, she delegated me to sort out a flat or an old people's home for Mrs Byers. Not too close to Hampstead, though.

Geraldine would of course have made these arrangements herself, but she was going to be too busy on her novel to afford the time. Now that George had published a book (and Susannah Franks was talking to him about a sequel), it was important that Geraldine should actually finish a novel that year. His wife's winning of the Booker Prize, she told me with her usual ingenuous charm, would perhaps put George's achievements in a more realistic perspective.

MOON SHINE
by
Geraldine Byers

'My life has been the stuff of legend,' she says. And the sister stops checking her pay-packet for a moment; she looks across at the faded old woman, the dying woman. 'Mine, and all,' the sister says. 'Now why haven't you eaten up your lovely rissoles?'

I am a legend. And I should chronicle my legend, as a fitting climax to my life. I'd do it very well. Everyone has always admired my literary skills, just as they always recognized how beautiful I am: and modest, too. Cynthia Hardwick has got the lot, that's what they always said.

'They get these delusions,' the sister confides to her junior. The temperature chart clangs back on the end of the bed after consultation. 'Claim they've had some kind of fairytale life . . . and in fact it's been as boring as hell . . .'

I see my legend differently from you. All of us have different perceptions of the past. We may read from the same books, but what I read is not what you read. Our brains receive conflicting information, and process it differently. I know, precisely, my place in the scheme of things. I am, so far as my perception is concerned, the centre. Other people are only important in relation to me.

I was castigated for this point of view as a child. My sisters thought me selfish and arrogant; but they perceived me from the vantage-point of their own egocentricity. They criticized; I ignored.

My father, too. My father was irrelevant, a broken reed.

Summoned from the kitchen, aged about twelve, I am ordered by my father to lay out a plastic sheet, advised: 'I'm expecting company and, knowing the sort of people they are, I think a lot of coloured water and foam could get splashed about, so please cover the furniture.' Unabashed, I say: 'Do it yourself.'

Legend, like history, is a sound made up of many voices. My father contributes to my legend, so do my sisters, my godmother, Bouton, and the other person more important than any of them. But I will not reveal his name yet, preferring to tease out my narrative, to keep changing from first person to third person, from the past to the present, the present to the future. I will do my duty in matching my pace to the slow accretion of legend, the build-up of its layers from a variety of sources over a very long time, like Mesozoic and Triassic rock formations.

There is a mummy of a cat in the Egyptian section of the British Museum, which I once contemplated with Quinten, long after the midnight encounter which divided my life as sharply as a switch snaps light from darkness. How should I describe Quinten? There are many ways of doing it, many lines of his characteristics which can be drawn, to converge and narrow down his personality to a cross-hatched area of increasing intensity. To define him thus would be in keeping with my multilayered narrative style. But since he is completely irrelevant to my legend, I don't think I'll bother.

'She's rambling,' says the young nurse, pausing for a moment in her folding of rubber sheets.

'Happens when they get to that age,' the sister whispers. 'They get confused about the past and the present. She doesn't know what day it is, poor old duck.'

There are no seats on the terrace. Free French, British naval officers, Sephardic Jews, fezzed Egyptians all contribute to the Babel. Suffragis edge between pushed-back chairs, trays of drinks held high. Cynthia cannot find a seat. It's very crowded, she thinks. Cairo is always crowded. A man rises to offer her a seat, a drink, a share of his bed perhaps. She is, after all, as she keeps telling everyone, very beautiful.

She accepts the chair and the drink, which is where she intends to draw the line. The man doesn't know this yet, and she isn't going to tell him for a while. He is Lieutenant Bouton of the Free French. He's not to know that he isn't the one man she wants, the man she hasn't met yet, but for whom the intensity of her feelings already frightens her.

144

As white-sailed feluccas skim across the water which the sunset washes with pinks and golds, Lieutenant Bouton thinks he's still in with a chance.

Coming back to the same scene in the packaged eighties, the terrace is still crowded, but now it is the terrace of a Hilton. The multilingual babble is still there, but the accents are American, German, Swedish, Dutch, Japanese, Australian, voices rich and idle enough to afford tourism. Cynthia sits apart from them. They are dreadful people, people of no culture. They do not know, or even seek, the real Egypt. For them it is only there to be portioned up and freeze-packed into their cameras. These are not people with whom she could have an intelligent conversation about Java Man and Australopithecus, the repercussions of the Hungarian Uprising or the problems of historiography. She ignores them.

'There must be something you want,' says Charlie, his gesture encompassing the rows of stalls, the hanging rugs, the scarab rings, the leather pouffes, the brass jugs.

'Yes, there must,' Cynthia murmurs, not concentrating, distracted by the lightheadedness of being with him.

He stops at the mouth of a dark shop, from whose doorway lianas of leather slippers trail down. 'How about a pair of these?'

'Yes,' says Cynthia, 'yes.'

The proprietor is instantly all over them, tape-measure at the ready, slippers flying as they are offered and discarded. She finds a pair that fit. Charlie pays for them. She slips them on, dropping her hard English shoes into her bag.

Charlie's hand finds her. 'I've given you the slippers. That means I'm part of your life. If you ever lose them – even one of them – I'm no longer part of your life.'

She smiles at him. Gharries clop past, trams clang by. She feels warm, even – a rare feeling for a nature as complex as hers – happy. She knows the sex will be good later.

The characters are coming together; the roll-call is nearly complete. A few late stragglers to be rounded up, then the story can begin. For the moment we are just going through the preliminaries, sorting approaches to the legend, deciding which way to proceed: whether to go next to another flashback, or a flashforward, whether to use the first person or the third; the present tense, the past – or even, why not, give ourselves a real intellectual thrill with a quick burst of the future conditional. When you are extraordinarily intelligent, you can derive enormous pleasure from playing with narrative structures like this. And if you ever hear of readers who are less than riveted by the process, you can comfort yourself with the knowledge that they're not as intelligent as you are.

Everything will fall into place, don't worry. My legend will be told, every piece of the jigsaw fitting, punctiliously, painstakingly, relentlessly intelligently, and quite slowly.

1988

Unfortunately, Geraldine didn't quite finish writing *Moon Shine* before the result of the 1988 Booker Prize was announced, and obviously, once she knew that Peter Carey had won with his *tour de force, Oscar and Lucinda*, she had to get George to pay for her to go to Australia for a month or two, so it wasn't until February 1989 that she was able to settle down to her new book.

This time, though Peter Carey had set her a fairly difficult target by the inordinate length of his prize-winning novel, she was determined to get the book finished. And in this ambition she was encouraged by Susannah Franks. The editor had been round for dinner at the Hampstead house one evening to discuss George's third book, *Chemicals from Nature: the Herbal Alternative*, and the conversation had quite quickly got round to Geraldine's writing. (I was in the kitchen washing up, but I could hear every word through the hatch!)

'Now George is up and running,' Susannah had said tactfully, 'I really wish we could publish something of yours.'

Geraldine gave a little, self-deprecating, suffering shrug.

'But you haven't actually got anything completed, have you? So I'm afraid — '

'I have a great deal of material very near completion, but . . .' Geraldine sighed, 'it is a mark of the true creative artist never to be wholly satisfied with his or her *oeuvre.*'

'Oh, sod that!' said Susannah. 'A book that's not finished is as bloody useless as one that hasn't been started. A writer has to be extremely eminent – and dead – to get something unfinished published.'

Geraldine shook her head at the sadness of this undoubted truth.

'What's the problem? Do you run out of ideas?'

A patronizing laugh greeted this simplistic approach. 'Oh, if only it were as uncomplicated as that, Susannah. No, no, my ideas teem in my imagination like young salmon.' She wasn't quite sure how apposite this image was, so moved hastily on. 'No, the *content* of my books is never a problem. My difficulty always comes with homing in on the proper *style* in which to present that content.'

Susannah looked blank. 'Well, surely the only possible style you can write in is your own style. I mean, writing's an expression of you, so your style is you. I'd have thought that was very straightforward . . . for a writer who's got any kind of personality at all.'

'Susannah, how easy you make it sound! I can tell why you're an editor and not a writer – you can *sym*pathize with the creative process, but you cannot *em*pathize with it. Writing is a long journey of self-discovery, and finding one's own style is only one part of that journey.'

'Are you saying that you have tried writing in a variety of different styles?'

Geraldine tried not to smile at the naïvete of the question. 'You could say that, Susannah. Yes, you could say that.'

'Why?'

Geraldine did not yet feel ready to reveal to the world the strategy to win the Booker Prize which had dominated her creative life for nearly twenty years. 'As I say, stripping off the layers of myself to find my own authentic voice.'

'Oh. So you actually have examples of half-written novels all done in different styles?'

'Cupboards full of them.'

'Good heavens.'

'Some wonderful writing . . .' Geraldine sighed nobly. 'But you try to get one of the new breed of modern editors interested in reading that kind of stuff.'

Susannah Franks looked embarrassed. 'Oh, I wouldn't say . . . I'm sure, given the right circumstances, the right person would, er . . .'

'Oh, very well. If you insist,' said Geraldine, and called out to me in the kitchen, 'Mary, could you go and get all my unfinished manuscripts from the cupboard in my workroom?'

Susannah proved rather slower than might have been wished in reading the cardboard boxes of orange- and pink-covered school exercise books and sheets of form feeds that had been thrust on her, but Geraldine was pleased to have her work at least being considered. She had been too reticent, too falsely modest in the past. There was now a strong possibility that Susannah would recognize the enormous merit in her unfinished efforts, and urge her to complete all of them.

Yes, it would of course be very hard work, but, if it was necessary, Geraldine was prepared to make the sacrifice. She did rather like the idea of her extensive private back-list suddenly bursting into print. The impact, she conjectured to me one morning over coffee, would not be dissimilar to that caused by the posthumous publication of Gerard Manley Hopkins' poems.

But Susannah's strictures about the necessity of finishing books were taken to heart. It was a regrettable necessity that the world worked in such a facile way, but Geraldine resigned herself to its imperfections and wrote every hour God gave to complete her extravagant Australian saga. She only broke off a couple of times a day to ring Susannah with news of her progress.

Geraldine had noticed, after the first few months, that her editor's manner had become increasingly testy each time she rang, but put this down to some trouble in Susannah's private life. Young girls always got themselves into such emotional twists, and it couldn't be a lot of fun trying to conduct a reasonable love-life in the AIDS-threatened eighties. Geraldine did feel rather privileged to have enjoyed the sexual freedom of earlier decades.

One day in May 1989, however, the explanation for Susannah's short temper was made clear. Geraldine had just rung through to Abrams & Willis for the second time that day to tell her editor about the four paragraphs she had completed since lunch when Susannah, unaccountably, shouted, 'Oh, for Christ's sake, fuck off!'

'I beg your pardon?' said Geraldine, shocked.

'Look, I've got more important things to do than listen to a word-by-word running commentary on your fucking book!'

'But editors are meant to take an interest in their authors' writing – that's what the job's about. And the book I'm working on's going to be a real *tour de force*.'

'I hope not. When critics use the expression "*tour de force*" about a book, all they mean is that it's too fucking long.'

'Listen, Susannah, if Abrams & Willis are hoping to publish my next book, I'm afraid I'm going to expect a rather more gracious — '

'There's a serious question mark over whether Abrams & Willis are going to publish another single fucking word ever again!'

'What do you mean?'

'Don't you read the bloody papers? We've been taken over.'

'Yes, I know you have. A few years ago P & L took over the whole of — '

'Yes, but, as of this morning P & L have been taken over.'

'Who by?'

'Some fucking Australian!'

'Good heavens,' said Geraldine, thinking of her book. 'They get everywhere.'

It must have been brewing for some time. And at least now she knew the reason why Susannah had been so tetchy with her on the phone recently.

Geraldine heard more about the takeover from George that evening. It had not been pleasant. All happened very quickly, and Maurice Ashby had been out on his ear within twenty-four hours. Maurice

Ashby wasn't clear about his future. None of the employees in any of the P & L conglomerate were clear about their future.

George said he was considering the idea of channelling some of the huge profits from his Green books into setting Maurice up on his own again. Maybe go in with him as a full-time partner. In spite of all the takeovers, he reckoned there was still room for efficient independent publishers. Still, early days to be thinking of that . . .

Geraldine liked the idea. George had done everything else for her since they'd married; it'd make sense if he published her Booker Prize-winning novel, too.

She continued to work hard and, before even the shortlist for the 1989 Prize was announced, she *finished* her novel.

Geraldine Byers summoned George and me into her workroom. She flicked through the neat computer-printed sheets, glowing with the satisfaction of the realized artist. Every now and then she stopped to read a bit out to us so that we could admire her skill.

CHARMING AND CINDA
by
Geraldine Byers
112
Glass Footwear

That the first product of Cinda's glassworks was a pair of slippers was for her not just a manufacturing achievement but also a justification, i.e. proof that she could make a go of the business. It would be easy to see the fact that slippers were the first artefacts as an indication that she wished to demonstrate the durability and practical applications of glass, and there would be some truth in that. But the opposite is also true, i.e. by making a pair of slippers she was demonstrating the spirituality, the transcendence if you like, of glass, its ability to bestow an almost alchemical sparkle on mundane objects.

You need not ask me how a glass slipper is made, because I can't tell you. But I do know what a glass slipper looks like. The surviving one of the pair which came into my great-grandfather's possession sits on the desk in front of me as I write (my pen scratching across the page), and every now and then I pick it up, feel its smooth surface with my hand, sense the incredible strength of its construction. I don't know the details of the blower's skills required to achieve this strength, the precise calculations needed to balance the forces of physics and channel the toughness of the glass into sole, heel, toecap and upper – you just take my word for the fact that it works. You could take a sledgehammer to this slipper – my father tried it once, wielding the instrument with considerable trepidation – and it would not shatter.

150

I am not suggesting that the possibility of manufacturing glass slippers was the main reason why Cinda purchased the glassworks, but it is clear that the idea was rooted at an early stage in her life, long before she came to Sydney, long before her preoccupation with gambling, long before her bizarre encounter with Charming, possibly from the time she was in her cradle, over which dangled a small chandelier, whose unlit but chiming lozenges, refracting light into spectrums, may have impressed on the infant mind the thought whose imprint, like the fossil foothole of an obsolescent dinosaur, endured through her childhood, and flowered into her magnificent obsession, the realization that glass, transparent, impermeable, at once material and immaterial, can be a symbol for more or less anything.

'Then there are a lot more chapters like that,' said Geraldine, 'you know, ranging widely across England and Australia . . .'

'It's terrific stuff, love,' said George. 'Now shall we go down and have a drink?'

'Well, no. There's one other bit I'd like to read you.'

'Ah.'

310

Floor Polish

That Cinda was lonely did not arise simply because she had cut herself off from Society, in part by her eccentricities, her singularity of dress, bizarre hair-styles and habit of talking about glass all the time, and also by her midnight encounter with Charming, behaviour calculated to raise unforgiving eyebrows on the faces of those in Sydney she cared least about; the loneliness was exacerbated by her parting from Charming. Now not only did she lack the company of people whose company she did not want, she also lacked the company of the one strange red-headed stick-insect she did care about.

She channelled her energy into polishing the floor. As she did so, she made plans. All her plans were about glass. Now she had only one glass slipper, her mind boiled with visions of new glass artefacts, sombre structures whose implications she did not like to investigate.

She would build herself a glass coffin.

A glass catafalque to house it.

A glass mauseoleum.

A glass necropolis.

Fortunately, she put off the implementation of these ominous plans, and busied herself with floor polish. The smell of it in the house was overpowering. She thought of floor polish as the incense of her glass funeral.

'What do you think, George?'

'Still great stuff.'

'There's lots more of it.'

'I'm sure there is. How about that drink now? Mary, what do you say to — ?'

'Just listen to this bit first,' said Geraldine.

'Oh.'

430
Be Not Righteous Over Much

Until he had the ill-fated idea of returning the glass slipper to its rightful owner, Charming's faith had been relatively simple. God always knew what his servant, that one poor, misshapen shaving from the almighty sculpture of the world, should be doing at any given time. In the past, Charming's only problem had been to interpret God's intentions for him. But, as he laboured through the bush, checking the horny, calloused tick-ridden feet of every woman he met, feeling the sweat trickle down his sides till it caked at his waistband, antagonized by mosquitoes, sandpapered by dust, stabbed at by piles, nauseated by the pervasive smell of shit and fetid mud, he had to reassess his relationship with his religion.

He prayed: Oh God, what the hell have I let myself in for?

'There are a lot more chapters about, you know, the privations of travel through the bush.'

'Are there really? Well, well,' said George.

'What do you think of it, Mary?'

'It's wonderful, Geraldine,' I said.

'And you, George? What do you think?'

'I think it's a real *tour de force*, love. Now shall we — '

'Just want to read you the end bit.'

'Ah.'

576
A Fitting Conclusion

By the time Charming had tried the glass slipper on Cinda's foot, to find it a snug and perfect fit, he was full of sin, remorse, sexual guilt, paranoia, nausea, sunburn, laudanum, alcohol, dreams, religion, memories and apathy. He decided he'd never really wanted to get married anyway, took the slipper back, and wandered off into the bush.

In November 1989 Susannah Franks took her to lunch at the Groucho Club to talk about the book. This suited Geraldine well; she liked being part of what she thought of as the glitzy end of publishing. The launch for George's second book had been at the Groucho. Martin Amis and Kazuo Ishiguro were supposed to have been there, though Geraldine hadn't been introduced to either of them.

Susannah had survived the first *putsch* at P & L after the Australian takeover and was continuing in her old job. 'They *say* there won't be any effect on editorial policy,' she confided darkly, as the two sat down in the bar with their drinks. 'They *say* Abrams & Willis will be allowed to continue in exactly the same way as before. Huh, I'll believe that when it happens. They've brought in a new editorial director. Born in Melbourne, would you believe. I don't know, fucking Australians get everywhere.' She nodded a greeting to Carmen Callil and Clive James who had just entered the club. 'Have you heard anything of Maurice Ashby?'

'Well, you know my husband George was trying to set up a new publishing house with him?'

'Yes, I'd heard. Anything coming of it?'

'I don't know. It's slow. Trying to get the capital together and . . . We'll see.'

'Hm.'

During lunch they talked about books. Geraldine Byers was in her element. She was, after all, a literary figure; she could think of nothing better than sitting over lunch in the Groucho Club talking about books.

It was only when they'd both indulged in bread and butter pudding and were settling down to the cafetière and the Armagnacs that Susannah Franks brought up the subject of Geraldine's book.

She didn't like it.

She didn't see any chance of Abrams & Willis publishing it.

Come to that, she didn't see any chance of any publisher in the history of the universe publishing it.

She had also looked through all of the writing in the orange and pink-covered school exercise books. And the most recent stuff on the form-feeds. She didn't think any of that was publishable either.

'I was not surprised,' Geraldine told me when she returned to Hampstead after lunch. 'I had always suspected a certain coarseness in Susannah Frank's intellect, and now my suspicions have been confirmed.'

'Yes,' I said. I was very impressed by the way Geraldine was taking it. There was a wonderful glow of martyrdom about her thin face. 'Aren't you depressed, though, by the reaction?'

She laughed a little, bitter laugh. 'My dear Mary, it has been the fate of writers from time immemorial to be misunderstood, reviled and undervalued. Uninformed criticism, like that which I have just heard from Susannah Franks, may hurt for a moment, but it can never harm the integrity of the true artist.'

'No, no, I suppose not.' I was silent for a moment. 'So will you offer *Charming and Cinda* to another publisher?'

'Perhaps. Perhaps not.' She looked momentarily wistful, as a new thought struck her. 'Maybe it will be my fate to be published posthumously, maybe my qualities will only be recognized after I have gone.'

'Oh, Geraldine . . .'

She smiled at me and then, as ever putting herself second, said, 'But I hope not. Otherwise you will not get the recognition you deserve from the publication of your biography.'

'Thank you, Geraldine.' I was almost overcome by the emotion of the moment. 'So . . .' I asked tentatively, 'you won't stop writing?'

She slowly shook her splendid head. 'A true writer has no choice in that matter, Mary. And I am Geraldine Byers, the writer. Oh, no, I will always write, so long as God grants life to my body and magic to my imagination. Now, you see, there is a new Booker Prize winner, a new style in which I must write my imperishable story . . .'

'Yes, yes. Oh, you're so brave, Geraldine.'

She laughed aside the compliment. 'It's not bravery, Mary. It's just the knowledge that I have something original to give to the world.'

'Oh.'

'That's what keeps me going. You see, the criticisms of someone like Susannah Franks don't bother me.'

'No?'

'No. Because they don't strike at what is truly distinctive about my writing.'

'Don't they?'

The splendid head was shaken once again. 'All she criticized was the styles in which I have written . . .'

'True.'

'Not the story I am telling.'

'No.'

'So I'm not worried. Until I find my own voice, all right, my style may here and there be slightly imitative, but the story I have to tell . . .' Geraldine Byers concluded with a smile of quiet satisfaction, 'at least there's no question about whether or not that's original, is there?'

'No,' I said. 'No, there isn't.'